D1606371

WORLD BANK STAFF OCCASIONAL PAPERS

NUMBER TWENTY-THREE

Shlomo Reutlinger
Marcelo Selowsky

Malnutrition and Poverty

Magnitude and Policy Options

PUBLISHED FOR THE WORLD BANK
The Johns Hopkins University Press
Baltimore and London

Library of Congress Cataloging in Publication Data

Reutlinger, Shlomo.
    Malnutrition and poverty.

    (World Bank staff occasional papers; no. 23)
    Includes bibliographical references.
    1. Nutrition policy. 2. Underdeveloped areas—
Nutrition. I. Selowsky, Marcelo, joint author.
II. Title. III. Series.
TX359.R48   362.5   76–17240
ISBN 0–8018–1868–0 pbk.

The most recent editions of *Catalog of Publications,* describing the full range
of World Bank publications, and *World Bank Research Program,* describing
each of the continuing research programs of the Bank, are available
without charge from:

WORLD BANK
PUBLICATIONS UNIT
1818 H STREET, N.W.
WASHINGTON, D.C. 20433
U.S.A.

Foreword

I would like to explain why the World Bank does research work and why this research is published. We feel an obligation to look beyond the projects that we help finance toward the whole resource allocation of an economy and the effectiveness of the use of those resources. Our major concern, in dealings with member countries, is that all scarce resources—including capital, skilled labor, enterprise, and know-how—should be used to their best advantage. We want to see policies that encourage appropriate increases in the supply of savings, whether domestic or international. Finally, we are required by our Articles, as well as by inclination, to use objective economic criteria in all our judgments.

These are our preoccupations, and these, one way or another, are the subjects of most of our research work. Clearly, they are also the proper concern of anyone who is interested in promoting development, and so we seek to make our research papers widely available. In doing so, we have to take the risk of being misunderstood. Although these studies are published by the Bank, the views expressed and the methods explored should not necessarily be considered to represent the Bank's views or policies. Rather, they are offered as a modest contribution to the great discussion on how to advance the economic development of the underdeveloped world.

ROBERT S. MCNAMARA
President
The World Bank

Contents

Tables

Figures

Preface

Only in recent years has the problem of malnutrition been viewed as a development problem—as not only a consequence of underdevelopment but a contributing factor to it, a drag on the potential from which better nutrition might be provided. Since 1973 the World Bank has been examining nutrition in the context of its own programs and has taken preliminary action on several fronts, including operational activities.

Malnutrition and Poverty presents the conclusions of a first large research effort in the World Bank to determine the global dimension of malnutrition in low-income countries and to investigate the economic dimensions of certain policy interventions by governments. The authors take explicit account of the close association between maldistribution of existing and projected food supplies and the incidence of malnutrition. In doing so, they have been able to improve on existing estimates of the dimension of the problem, and they demonstrate conclusively that the roots of malnutrition and policy palliatives cannot be assessed without explicit consideration of the distribution of food among different groups in the population.

In short, the authors conclude that malnutrition "is not likely to go away in the normal course of development"; on the contrary, the situation may under some circumstances get worse. Similarly, although there are strong links between the food problem (which has received much attention of late) and the malnutrition problem (which has received considerably less), the authors demonstrate that the malnutrition problem is not going to be solved simply by solving the aggregate food problem.

Deliberate policies and programs are called for, especially among nutritionally vulnerable groups. Of the alternatives examined, food programs oriented to target groups are regarded as more cost effective than general food price subsidies and outright income redistribution. The authors appreciate the difficulties that must be surmounted in implementing such programs, but conclude "they may offer the only hope for meeting the challenge of hunger amid plenty."

Although they recognize undeniable need for expansion of the total food supply, the authors point out that the food deficit is small relative to aggregate food availability. The nutrition deficit and the distribution needs this implies is a more difficult issue with which to deal. Unlike certain other recent statements on the food problem, theirs is not a pessimistic prognosis—except in the sense that the policies proposed to solve malnutrition problems are not now being adequately pursued. This volume is published in the hope that it will help bring about a better understanding of the problem and of what is required to meet it.

The original version of this research was one of several studies undertaken by a World Bank task force on urban poverty. In the process of improving on earlier drafts, the authors received useful comments by Graham Pyatt and Lance Taylor; they are especially grateful to Nanak Kakwani for his suggestions about the estimation of the income distribution data used in the study. The final manuscript was edited by Julia McGraw.

ALAN BERG
Senior Nutrition Adviser
Agriculture and Rural
Development Department

Washington, D.C.
June 1976

Malnutrition and Poverty

Magnitude and Policy Options

1

Introduction and Summary

MALNUTRITION is but one of several manifestations of poverty, yet its effects, as well as the policy instruments available to improve the nutritional status of populations, have distinctive features that deserve separate analysis.

First, nutrition is one of the main determinants of health, and health is now regarded as a desirable end in itself and distinct from the general objective of improving economic welfare. In this view the allocation of food and other health-preserving measures need not conform to the criteria normally used for allocating income and wealth in general. A society may have no minimum standard for income yet strive for minimum standards for health and nutrition for all its citizens. Similarly, a society may generally respect the sovereignty of family units over the allocation of their earnings but still take deliberate measures to bias allocations in favor of better nutrition for all or some members of the family.

Second, health and nutrition interventions have an impact on human capital formation, with implications for the future earnings of individuals and the growth in gross national product. The nutritional status of infants is perhaps the most important policy-induced determinant of the individual's initial physical condition, which in turn determines the effectiveness of further investment in human capital. Certain types of malnutrition during the working years appear to have a crucial influence on an individual's level of productivity.

On the policy side, the effectiveness of nutrition interventions depends heavily on the behavior of households in reaction to such policies. Households make the ultimate decision concerning nutri-

1

tional intake, and it is in this context that public policies must be designed. The problem of nutrition also has unique features in relation to supply decisions. The greater part of infrastructure services is usually provided directly by the government, yet in making public nutrition policies in most mixed economies it must be taken into account that the private sector will ultimately be the main source of food supply. In other words, nutrition policies face a more complex situation in that private decisionmaking—as regards both supply and demand—plays a more dominant role than in other types of public intervention.

That undernutrition is a function of absolute poverty is self-evident. But estimates of the global magnitude of the calorie deficits in developing countries have usually been made by reference to highly aggregated per capita data. Moreover, policies to curtail undernutrition often employ instruments—such as those which increase per capita food production and consumption—that do not differentiate among beneficiaries.

This study consists of two parts: an assessment of the nature and magnitude of undernutrition in the developing countries, with special reference to income distribution; and a theoretical analysis of the cost effectiveness of some policy instruments to reduce under-nutrition of target groups in urban areas.

MAGNITUDE OF THE WORLD CALORIE DEFICIT

Chapter 2 discusses the nature and extent of undernutrition. It reviews the extent of undernutrition in the developing countries, as measured by the gap, or deficit, between the intake and the physiological requirements of calories. The need of deriving such deficit estimates by reference to income groups is emphasized inasmuch as national averages underestimate the relevant deficit by pooling calorie surpluses and deficits. An attempt has been made here to compute deficits by income groups by using income distribution data for different regions and applying plausible estimates of the calorie-income relation.

Based on average calorie consumption data in the mid-1960s, it is estimated that 56 percent of the population in developing countries (some 840 million people) had calorie-deficient diets in excess of 250 calories a day. Another 19 percent (some 290 million people) had deficits of less than 250 calories a day.

It is noteworthy that the above estimates are not especially sensitive to recommended levels of calorie requirements. This is important, since the particular level of calorie requirement used in making estimates in this and most other studies has recently come into question as overstating the true requirements. Although a lower requirement level—say, by 10 percent—would indeed wipe out the undernutrition problem when undernutrition is measured as the difference between total regionwide calorie availability and requirements, such a reduction in the level of requirements would reduce only marginally the size of the undernourished population when measured by the method used in this study.

The first two columns of Table 1 show earlier estimates of calorie deficits based on regional and country averages. The third column contains the estimates by income groups derived in this study.

Estimates based on regional averages are unrealistically low because they contain the implicit assumption that surpluses in some countries compensate for deficits in other countries—and, similarly, that within countries, surpluses of some income groups compensate for deficits of others. The latter assumption is also implicit in estimates obtained by summing the average deficits of all deficit countries. Total deficit estimates based on country averages therefore also underestimate the true deficit.

From Table 1 it may be concluded that estimates of world calorie deficits given here (by the use of a mid-figure of the daily deficit of 419 thousand million calories) are one-third higher than the ones obtained through existing country average data. A better appreciation of a calorie deficit of this order of magnitude may be conveyed by noting that 400 thousand million calories a day are equivalent to approximately 38 million metric tons of food grain a year—a figure equal to 4 percent of the world production of cereals in the mid-1960s.

By the use of the same analytical framework for estimation, the

Table 1. Daily Calorie Deficits in Developing Countries, 1965
(Thousand millions of calories)

Region	Regional averages	Country averages	Income group averages
Latin America	0	19	32–74
Asia	202	213	225–283
Middle East	19	32	32–45
Africa	48	50	61–86
Total	269	314	350–488

Source: Table 9.

calorie deficit for 1965 was projected forward to 1975 and 1990. With per capita income in all income groups growing at approximately the current rate of overall per capita income growth and per capita food supply growing just enough to meet the demand generated by the income growth, the total calorie deficit would remain virtually unchanged by 1990. The absolute number of people suffering from undernutrition would be higher, but their proportion of the total population would decline. The per capita daily deficit in the afflicted population would decline from approximately 350 calories in 1965 to approximately 240 calories in 1990.

Were income distribution to remain unchanged, extremely high rates of growth in the demand for and supply of food would be required to achieve per capita growth rates of food consumption that would eliminate the calorie deficits in the lowest income classes. The necessary growth rates in per capita income needed to sustain such growth in demand are not likely to be achieved. Furthermore, it would require a rate of growth in food production and consumption that could be achieved only if large subsidies were paid to maintain high incentive prices to farmers and low food prices to consumers. A realistic solution to the problem therefore must lie in target-group–oriented programs specifically designed to allow people of low income to achieve minimal standards of adequate nutrition.

Breastfeeding and Infant Malnutrition

Chapter 2 also reviews briefly some aspects of infant undernutrition, with particular reference to changes in income and breastfeeding. An analysis of a comprehensive nutrition survey of low-income families in Calcutta shows that the nutrition of all age groups improves with rising income. Although the nutrient-income elasticities for young infants are higher than for adults, this does not mean that infant undernutrition is resolved with improvement in income. In fact, the opposite can be true if it is assumed that higher incomes are achieved partly through the mother obtaining employment, with the consequent partial sacrifice of breastfeeding. The same Calcutta data show that the marginal propensity of spending on infants' diets from additional family income is extremely low, on the order of 5 percent. A low marginal propensity is consistent with a high income elasticity out of family income if, as is the case, only a small fraction of the total expenditure is devoted to childfeeding in the first place. Yet calculations about the loss of breastfeeding and the cost of replacing the equivalent nutrients suggest that about 50 percent of the mother's earnings would need to be spent on the infant for the sheer maintenance of its nutritional health. Clearly, higher per capita incomes not only may fail to reduce but, on the contrary, may increase infant undernutrition.

Cost Effectiveness of Alternative Policies

Chapters 3 and 4 contain an analysis of the cost effectiveness of various policies aimed at improving the nutritional status of the urban target population. Policies may be divided between country-wide and target-group–oriented policies. The countrywide policy considered is A GENERAL PRICE SUBSIDY on a particular food for the entire urban population. Target-group–oriented programs considered are A FOOD PRICE SUBSIDY, A FOOD STAMP PROGRAM, and A STRAIGHTFORWARD INCOME TRANSFER for the undernourished population.

Cost effectiveness is defined as the fiscal cost per additional unit of food or specific nutrient consumed by the undernourished group. For every policy, two scenarios were considered: first, that the additional food is obtained at a constant price, as in the case of a country that imports food; and, second, that the additional food requirement causes its price to rise. Cost effectiveness in terms of a nutrition objective for the target groups is obviously not the only criterion whereby a preferred policy is established. A general food price subsidy may be justified as an instrument for keeping down wages and wage-push inflation. Food price subsidies may also be advocated to increase farm income. Target-group–oriented programs may have multiple objectives: to increase food consumption and to increase the consumption of other commodities and services. In the final analysis, political feasibility is important in selecting the optimal policy.

As might be expected, a general food price subsidy is the least cost-effective policy for eliminating undernutrition in the target population. On the assumption that the target population's share of total consumption of the food is 20 percent and its demand elasticity is 1.0, it will cost approximately $5 to provide them with $1 worth of food—and this is probably the most favorable case.[1] If the target group's demand elasticity is 0.5, it will cost approximately $12 to provide the same amount of food. The program will be even

---

1. The dollars referred to throughout the book are U.S. dollars.

more expensive if the additional food requirement leads to a higher food price. If the supply elasticity is 1.0 and the demand elasticity of the nontarget population is 0.5, it will cost $9 in the first case and $18 in the second. These illustrative but not unrepresentative figures should give second thoughts to those who seek the answer to undernutrition through general food price subsidies, either in the form of a direct subsidy or of subsidized agricultural inputs.

Target-group–oriented policies are generally more cost effective. But only a food stamp program that provides participants with a claim for food in excess of their current consumption—at a cost equivalent to their food expenditure without the program—could be expected to provide $1 of food consumption per $1 program cost. The cost effectiveness of a price subsidy to the target group is approximately inversely proportional to the group's demand elasticity for the food: that is, it would cost about $1.33 if the elasticity were 0.75. Similarly, the cost effectiveness of a straight income transfer is approximately inversely proportional to the target group's marginal propensity to spend on the food: that is, the cost would be about $2 if the marginal propensity were 0.5. When the additional food requirements for the program cause the price of food to rise, all target-group–oriented programs become only slightly less cost effective. The additional food requirement of such a program is not likely to be large (as it is in general food price subsidies), and to an extent will be compensated by a decline in food consumption by the nontarget population.

In any case, the actual cost effectiveness of target-group–oriented programs may be less than is implied by the actual calculations. In reality, several kinds of leakages occur. A great deal of ingenuity is required to assure that all the benefits from a target-oriented food program reach only the intended beneficiaries. Middlemen and administrators may divert the subsidized food to the regular market. Some of the concessionary food may be purchased by people outside the target group. Where there is a food price subsidy, the participants may resell some food at the unsubsidized price. If this were to happen, the food price subsidy program would become only as effective as an income transfer.

Actual food assistance programs in developing countries often cannot be classified as belonging strictly to one particular policy as analyzed in this study. For instance, a general food price subsidy may be applied to a commodity that is in fact primarily consumed by the target group. Public stores, selling food rations at a subsidized price (a method popular in several Asian countries), may cater primarily but not exclusively to the target group. The cost effectiveness of food rations would depend on the size of the rations. If the ration supplies less than the amount of food participants would be consuming without the program, the cost effectiveness is no more than could be achieved with a straight income transfer. If the ration supplies all the food the participants would want to consume at the subsidized price, the cost effectiveness is the same as with a price subsidy.

CONCLUSION

Malnutrition is unlikely to disappear in the normal course of development: that is, in the course of normal per capita income growth, even with greater emphasis on expansion of food production—barring, of course, unusual technological breakthroughs. On the contrary the situation may worsen if present higher energy cost, leading to higher cost of food production, is not fully compensated by higher agricultural productivity. Only policies deliberately designed to reallocate food or income can eliminate undernutrition. Target-group–oriented food programs in urban areas and programs to assist low-income farm families to increase and stabilize production of food for their own consumption can be more cost effective than outright income distribution. Although there must be no illusions about the difficulties to be surmounted in implementing such programs, they may offer the only hope for meeting the challenge of hunger amid plenty.

2

The Nature and Extent
of Malnutrition

JUST AS THE EDUCATIONAL LEVEL of a population should ideally be measured by its educational achievements and not by its exposure to, and use of, educational inputs, so malnutrition should ideally be defined by its consequences, such as health status, rather than by nutrient intake. In practice, it is difficult to define objective indicators of consequences, and it is even more difficult to collect and interpret relevant data.

The consequences of undernutrition are, first, poor bodily and mental health, which in turn causes physical suffering and mental anguish; and, second, low productivity, with effects on private and national levels of consumption and on accumulation of wealth. Such indexes of underachievement clearly are not easily defined or measured objectively. It is possible to measure mortality rates and the incidence of some diseases for children, as well as certain indexes of bodily and mental growth, and to attribute these with fair certainty to inadequate nutrition. In some cases, productivity data can be obtained and low productivity traced to inadequate nutrition.[1] But by and large the concepts are not developed, and

---

1. For attempts to associate productivity with infant malnutrition and iron deficiency in workers, see, respectively, Marcelo Selowsky and Lance Taylor, "The Economics of Malnourished Children: An Example in Disinvestment in Human Capital," *Economic Development and Cultural Change,* 22 (October 1973): 17–30; and S. S. Basta and A. Churchill, "Iron Deficiency Anemia and the Productivity of Adult Males in Indonesia," World Bank Staff Working Paper no. 175 (Washington, D.C.: World Bank, 1974).

data are not available to provide a global picture of undernutrition on the basis of indexes of nutrition-related achievement.

It is even more difficult to deduce from indexes of nutrition-related underachievement the particular explanatory variables that can be manipulated by policy measures and to isolate their effect from effects of other environmental variables conditioning those indexes of underachievement.

With these reservations as background, we turn to the definition and measurement of deficiencies in the intake of nutrients as indicators of malnutrition.

CALORIES VERSUS SPECIFIC NUTRIENTS

The most promising indicator for measuring the extent of nutritional inadequacies in large population groupings is the deficit in dietary energy measured in calories. Calorie requirement standards can be determined with fair precision for specified populations. In addition to the direct ill effects of calorie-deficient diets on physical and mental health and the ability to perform normal activity, calorie deficiency also often signals insufficient intake of specific nutrients such as proteins, minerals, and vitamins. This is particularly true when the theory is accepted that in such cases part of the protein is used as energy. In nutrition surveys based on 7,000 households in four states of India, about 50 percent of those persons with calorie deficiencies also had inadequate protein intake. By contrast, only 5 percent of the households without calorie deficiencies had inadequate intake of protein.[2]

Protein consumption is an unreliable indicator of malnutrition because generally applicable standards of requirements are more difficult to define. Protein utilization depends on many specific conditions such as environmental health, amino acid composition of the protein, and whether part of the protein is used as calories in calorie-deficient diets. Diseases of undernutrition as a result of inadequacies of specific nutrients are more often a local or age-specific problem than is the widespread phenomenon of large population groupings' consuming insufficient calories.

2. P. V. Sukhatme, "Incidence of Protein Deficiency in Relation to Different Diets in India," *British Journal of Nutrition* 24 (1970): 447–87.

POPULATIONWIDE EVIDENCE ON CALORIE DEFICITS

How many people in the developing countries today suffer from a deficit in calorie intake? This seems a simple question given the vast amount of data on food consumption that has been collected around the world. Yet existing data and analyses remain highly unsatisfactory.

Estimates of calorie deficiencies are usually based on two major data sources: surveys of household budget and food consumption and aggregate national food consumption data. Household food consumption surveys rarely cover all segments of the population in sufficient detail to derive aggregate estimates that are reconcilable with national food consumption data. Global estimates of calorie deficits and of the number of people afflicted are therefore made on the basis of comparisons between aggregate per capita calorie consumption and requirements in countries or regions. Such analyses clearly underestimate the true magnitude of the problem because of the unequal distribution of food among regions and countries and among people within countries. Such calculations imply—incorrectly—that calories consumed in excess of physiological requirements can be counted against the aggregate calorie requirements.[3]

As an illustration of the order of magnitude of the actual nutritional inadequacies when derived on the basis of income groups rather than country averages, it is instructive to review the case of Brazil. Based on family budget surveys in the early 1960s on a national sample and a reconciliation of these data with national food consumption data, the national average daily per capita consumption amounted to 2,566 calories, or a calculated excess over per capita requirements of about 116 calories. Yet analysis by income groups shows that approximately 44 percent of the total population

3. For example, the Food and Agriculture Organization (FAO) estimated average calorie consumption as a percent of requirements in 1970 as follows: 105 percent in Latin America, 94 percent in Asia, 93 percent in the Middle East, 92 percent in Africa, and 95 percent in all developing regions. (Source: United Nations, Economic and Social Council, Preparatory Committee of the World Food Conference, "Assessment of Present Food Situation" [E/ Conf./Prep./6] [Rome, 1974].) Based on the average of all developing regions, the total annual calorie deficit would seem to be approximately 180 thousand million units, or the equivalent of 20 million metric tons of grain. Alternatively, when the calorie deficits in deficit countries are added up, the total annual deficit amounts to approximately 260 thousand million calories.

Table 2. Calorie Consumption and Deficit by Income Groups, Brazil, 1960 [a]

Annual family income (new cruzeiros)	Population		Daily calorie consumption		Daily calorie deficit [a]	
	Number (thousands)	Percent of total	Amount (millions)	Percent of total	Per capita	Total (millions)
Under 100	3,583	5.05	5,172	2.87	1,006	3,604
100–149	4,873	6.87	8,847	4.91	634	3,089
150–249	12,235	17.25	25,940	14.41	330	4,037
250–349	10,197	14.37	23,378	12.98	157	1,601
350–499	11,145	15.71	28,293	15.71		
500–799	12,884	18.16	34,958	19.41		
800–1,199	7,198	10.14	22,689	12.60		
1,200–2,499	6,840	9.65	23,022	12.78		
2,500 and over	1,986	2.80	7,800	4.33		
Total	70,941	100.00	180,099	100.00		12,331

Source: Fundacão Getúlio Vargas, *Food Consumption in Brazil: Family Budget Survey in Early 1960s* (Jerusalem: Israel Program for Scientific Translations, 1970), Tables 4, A.2, A.3, and A.4.

a. Deficits are defined as the difference between daily calorie requirements (2,450 calories) and actual consumption.

were calorie deficient. Brazil's daily calorie deficiency amounted to some 12 thousand million calories, or 7 percent of its population's actual calorie consumption. Without regard to distribution, Brazil's level of consumption could have been judged as more than adequate (see Table 2).

ESTIMATING CALORIE CONSUMPTION BY INCOME GROUPS

Any attempt to make a reasonable estimate of calorie deficits in the developing countries clearly must take explicit account of the unequal distribution of calorie consumption among income groups. In the absence of direct data on the number of people whose calorie intake is short by a known amount of their requirements, an indirect estimation procedure based on existing data might serve as a reasonable approximation of the true magnitudes involved.[4]

The basic strategy of the analysis consists of allocating the total

4. Household food consumption sample surveys for a few urban and rural populations are of course available. The data generated in these surveys, however, cannot be used directly for assessing the global dimension of food consumption by income groups without first reconciling the extrapolated data from such surveys and available data about national total food consumption.

known amount of calories consumed in each major region among eight income groups. For each region, observed per capita calorie consumption (C^o) consists of the weighted sum of per capita consumption by income groups (C_i); that is:

$$（1）\qquad C^o = \Sigma w_i C_i,$$

where the weights (w_i) are the shares of the region's population in each income group. The sum of the weights is 1. The relation between consumption and income (X_i) is specified to take on the semilogarithmic form:

$$（2）\qquad C_i = a + b \mathrm{Ln} X_i.$$

Equation (2) implies appropriately that the calorie income elasticity (μ) is a declining function of consumption (and income); that is:

$$（3）\qquad u_i = b / C_i.$$

Substituting equation (2) into equation (1) yields equation (4), which is used for estimating the per capita calorie consumption by income groups consistent with total calorie consumption:

$$（4）\qquad C^o = a + b \, \Sigma w_i \mathrm{Ln} X_i.$$

Observed per capita calorie consumption (C^o) and requirements (C^r) by major regions are shown in Table 3. Per capita regional consumption estimates were derived by aggregating each country's per capita calorie consumption, weighted by its share in the region's total population.[5] If the country estimates are not biased in one direction, the regional aggregates should be fairly precise, in spite of large errors in the country estimates of calorie consumption and population. The per capita calorie requirements data are regional estimates used by the Food and Agriculture Organization (FAO) of the United Nations.

The distribution of population shares receiving specified levels of per capita income, reported in Table 4, were estimated on the basis of income distribution data from thirty countries, accounting for 900 million people, or about 60 percent of the population. The sources of the data and the method used for transforming income share distributions into distributions of shares of the population falling within specified ranges of per capita income are given in Appendix B. Although these data are clearly of questionable pre-

---

5. The basic country data are provided in Appendix A.

Table 3. Daily per Capita Calorie Consumption and Requirements in Developing Countries, by Regions, 1965

Region	Calorie consumption (C^o)	Standard Calorie requirements (C^r)
Latin America	2,472	2,390
Asia	1,980	2,210
Middle East	2,315	2,450
Africa	2,154	2,350

Source: Appendix A.

cision, the numbers are sufficiently close to other estimates to have validity in the context of the present analysis.

Finally, estimates of the parameters in equation (4) are required. An estimate of b (the calorie income propensity) at once implies a value for a, since the object is to ensure that the equation is consistent with allocating the actually observed mean level of calorie consumption, (C^o); that is:

$$(5) \qquad a = C^o - b\Sigma w_i \mathrm{Ln} X_i.$$

Table 4. Income Distribution in Developing Countries, by Regions, 1965

Class [b]	Range	Mean (X_i)	Latin America	Asia	Middle East	Africa
I	Under 50	35	6.6	19.6	13.4	29.7
II	51–100	75	16.0	43.3	20.4	31.8
III	101–150	125	13.0	19.3	17.7	15.8
IV	151–200	175	10.7	8.3	11.4	8.4
V	201–250	225	8.6	4.0	8.1	4.9
VI	251–300	275	6.9	2.1	5.8	3.0
VII	301–350	325	5.6	1.3	4.3	1.9
VIII	Over 350	1,131	32.5	0	0	0
		1,119	0	2.1	0	0
		717	0	0	18.9	0
		908	0	0	0	4.5
Per capita income ($\bar{X}$)			474	120	246	136
Population (millions)			244	896	144	247

Per capita income [a]; Percentage of population

Source: Appendix B.
a. Income is in 1972 constant U.S. dollars.
b. For classes I to VII, the means are assumed values. The mean of the highest income group was calculated to satisfy the equation $\Sigma w_i X_i = \bar{X}$, $i = $ I . . . VIII.

As a first approach, the parameter b was estimated for each region with cross-country per capita calorie consumption and income data; that is, the equation estimated was:

$$(6) \qquad\qquad C_j = a + b\mathrm{Ln}X_j + \epsilon_j,$$

where C_j and X_j are country per capita calorie consumption and income. The results are presented in Table 5. The data and regression results obtained with alternative mathematical specifications are shown in Appendix C.

Several observations may be made about the appropriateness of using the parameter estimates obtained from cross-country statistical analysis. Less than 50 percent of the variability in calorie consumption is explained by income in all regions. As a direct consequence and the low number of observations, the precision of the b estimates is not very high, although in three of the four regions the coefficient is statistically significant. Moreover, the low predictive power of the estimating equation and a priori theory suggests that income alone cannot explain all the differences in consumption. Intercountry variation in income distribution, urbanization, relative food price, and sociocultural factors are additional explanatory variables.[6] To the extent that any of these omitted

---

6. Some attempt was made to take intracountry income distribution explicitly into account in estimating the relation between calorie consumption and income from cross-country data. The number of countries for which income distribution data are available, however, limits the number of observations. For the same fourteen countries in Latin America and ten countries in Asia and the Middle East combined, the comparable results were as follows:

Latin America

$C_j = 530 + 311\ (\Sigma w_{ij}\mathrm{Ln}X_{ij}) \qquad R^2 = 0.73$
       (3.7)

$C_j = -417 + 452\ \mathrm{Ln}X_j \qquad R^2 = 0.81$
         (4.8)

Asia and the Middle East

$C_j = 1388 + 163\ (\Sigma w_{ij}\mathrm{Ln}X_{ij}) \qquad R^2 = 0.50$
       (1.6)

$C_j = 1538 + 119\ \mathrm{Ln}X_j \qquad R^2 = 0.38$
       (1.2)

Because neither the precision nor the bias of the estimates was in a clear direction and the number of countries with explicit income distribution data is small, the specification of equation (6) in the text was considered preferable.

Table 5. Estimated Equations of per Capita Calorie Consumption
from Cross-country Data, by Regions, 1965

Region	Equation [a]	Coefficient of determination R^2	Elasticity at region's observed level of calorie consumption
Latin America	$C = -256 + 417\,LnX$ (4.1)	0.44	0.168
Asia	$C = 1191 + 188\,LnX$ (3.5)	0.46	0.095
Middle East	$C = 1700 + 96\,LnX$ (2.4)	0.15	0.041
Africa	$C = 1854 + 71\,LnX$ (0.6)	0.04	0.033

a. Figures in parentheses are t statistics.

variables are correlated with income, the calorie-income coefficient
estimates obtained by the oversimplified specification could be
biased. The net effect of such biases cannot be ascertained, however, without examination of additional data that are not readily
available.

Another disadvantage of using cross-country data for estimating
the parameters relevant to the estimation of calorie consumption
by income groups is the limited range of variation in countries' per
capita income as compared with variation in the income of individuals. Even if the estimating equation adequately reflects the
relation between consumption and income over the range of country
per capita incomes, it does not directly follow that the equation
is also appropriate for per capita incomes outside this range.

The plausibility of using the statistically estimated b coefficients
was further tested by using them in conjunction with the observed
calorie consumption and income distribution data in the respective regions. The resulting equations, implied calorie consumption
levels at low- and high-income levels and corresponding elasticities,
as well as the implied level of income needed for the consumption
of minimum calorie requirements, are shown in Table 6.

There are several nonstatistical criteria for judging the plausibility of calorie consumption functions. An acceptable function should
predict a level of calorie consumption consistent with the critical
minimum calorie requirements needed to sustain life at the lowest
prevailing income levels and also consistent with the purchasing
power of the corresponding lowest income. Calorie consumption

Table 6. Analysis of Calorie Consumption Equations Using Statistically Estimated Coefficients of Consumption Propensity, 1965

Region	Equation	Per capita income US$25		Per capita income US$3,000		Income needed to meet FAO calorie requirements (U.S. dollars)
		Calorie consumption	Elasticity	Calorie consumption	Elasticity	
Latin America	$C = 147 + 417\ LnX$	1,489	0.28	3,486	0.12	217
Asia	$C = 1139 + 188\ LnX$	1,744	0.11	2,644	0.07	298
Middle East	$C = 1830 + 96\ LnX$	2,139	0.04	2,599	0.04	638
Africa	$C = 1836 + 71\ LnX$	2,065	0.03	2,404	0.03	1,393

data collected in a large number of household surveys provide empirical evidence that low-income groups often subsist on as little as 50 percent of the recommended FAO calorie requirement levels.[7] The estimated low levels of calorie consumption predicted at $25 for Latin America and Asia are therefore plausible.[8] On the other hand, a diet containing more than 2,000 calories per day could be expected to cost nearly or in excess of $25 a year, and therefore the levels of calorie consumption implied by the Middle East and Africa equations are likely to be too high.[9]

Similarly, for high levels of income a plausible equation should predict calorie intakes that are not in excess or short of calorie levels implied by the food consumption pattern of high-income classes. The equation for Latin America seems more plausible based on that criterion than the equations for the other regions.

Another test of plausibility is the consistency of the implied elasticities with food income elasticity estimates provided in many food demand studies. Certainly the very low elasticities implied by the equations for the Middle East and Africa are not plausible. It should, of course, be expected that calorie elasticities be lower than food expenditure elasticities; as incomes rise, people turn to more expensive sources of calories—that is, foods containing more and higher quality nutrients per calorie and foods more palatable and convenient to prepare.[10] Nevertheless, for very low levels of

7. See, for instance, U.S., Agency for International Development, *A Study of Food Habits in Calcutta* (Calcutta: Hindustan Thompson Associates, 1972); and Fundacão Getúlio Vargas, *Food Consumption in Brazil.*

8. The difference between Latin America and Asia may be a direct consequence of the larger share of the population in Latin America residing in urban areas.

9. For instance, if all calories are supplied by a cereal, the daily grain equivalent would be approximately 600 grams. At a retail cost of 20 cents a kilogram, the annual cost of the diet would be $44.

10. Let calories (C) and the cost of calories (P) be a function of income, X, that is:

(1) $$C = C(X) \text{ and}$$

(2) $$P = P(X).$$

The respective income elasticities are then:

(3) $$E_c = C'(X) \cdot \frac{X}{C(X)} \text{ and}$$

(4) $$E_p = P'(X) \cdot \frac{X}{P(X)}.$$

Food expenditure (Y) can be expressed as the cost per calorie, $P(X)$, times the number of calories, $C(X)$; that is:

income, the calorie income elasticity should be expected to be significantly higher than zero. Several analyses of data obtained through household food consumption surveys have confirmed that calorie income elasticities in the range of 0.10 to 0.30 are consistent with observed behavior.[11]

A final test of the plausibility of the consumption equation is the implied level of income associated with the recommended level of calorie requirements. The statistically fitted equations for the Middle East and Africa clearly imply income levels far higher than would seem plausible.

In view of all the statistical and nonstatistical shortcomings of equations based on the b parameter estimated from cross-country data, two sets of calorie consumption functions were specified that, in our judgment, bracket the full range of functions consistent with data and observations from other studies. The equations and implied levels of consumption at low- and high-income levels are presented in Table 7.

The two sets of functions were specified with the property of having implicit calorie-income elasticities of 0.15 and 0.30, respectively, at each region's level of calorie requirements. Given that the expression of the elasticity is b/C the b coefficients vary among regions in direct proportion to their different levels of calorie requirements. It is reasonable to expect that people have a higher propensity to spend for calories at any given level of income when their physiological requirements are higher. A lower elasticity than 0.15 was ruled out simply because there is much empirical evidence from food market and household consumption studies indicating that the income elasticity should be significantly positive. A higher elasticity than 0.30 was seen to be inconsistent with the data, inasmuch as a higher elasticity would imply that large low-income

---

(5) $$Y = P(X) \cdot C(X).$$

The food expenditure income elasticity is:

(6) $$E_y = [P'(X) \cdot C(X) + C'(X) \cdot P(X)] \frac{X}{P(X)C(X)}.$$

Substituting equations (3) and (4) into (6) gives:

(7) $$E_y = E_p + E_c.$$

The last expression shows that the calorie income elasticity is the food expenditure elasticity minus the cost of calorie elasticity.

11. See, for example, Fundacão Getúlio Vargas, *Pesquisa Sobre Consumo Alimentos* (Instituto Brasileiro de Economia, 1975), pp. 192–95; D. Chernichovsky, "The Demand for Nutrition—an Economic Interpretation," (Washington, D.C.: World Bank, 1975; processed); and Table 17 in this book.

Table 7. Analysis of Calorie Consumption Equations Using Assumed Elasticities of 0.15 and 0.30 at Level of Calorie Requirements, 1965

Region	Equation	Implied per capita calorie consumption at per capita income of		Income needed to meet FAO calorie require-ment (U.S. dollars)
		US$25	US$3,000	
Elasticity at level of requirements: 0.15 [a]				
Latin America	$C = 471 + 359 \, LnX$	1,627	3,345	210
Asia	$C = 491 + 332 \, LnX$	1,560	3,149	177
Middle East	$C = 455 + 368 \, LnX$	1,640	3,401	226
Africa	$C = 574 + 353 \, LnX$	1,710	3,400	153
Elasticity at level of requirements: 0.30 [b]				
Latin America	$C = -1524 + 717 \, LnX$	784	4,217	235
Asia	$C = -997 + 663 \, LnX$	1,137	4,311	126
Middle East	$C = -1399 + 735 \, LnX$	967	4,486	188
Africa	$C = -1002 + 705 \, LnX$	1,267	4,643	116

a. The elasticity implied at US$25 per capita income is approximately 0.22 in all regions.
b. The elasticity implied at US$25 per capita income varies from 0.55 in Africa to 0.91 in Latin America.

segments of the population could subsist on consumption levels too low to sustain life.

Calorie consumption by income groups and population shares with the two consumption functions are shown in Figures 1 through 8. Total calorie deficit is represented by the shaded deficit area in each graph, multiplied by the region's population.

Table 8 contains a summary of the estimates of the number of people consuming insufficient calories and the total calorie deficit in the developing countries, corresponding with the two sets of consumption functions. Within the limits bracketed by the two sets of functions, the estimated size of the undernourished population does not vary significantly. The size of the population with a daily per capita calorie deficit in excess of 250 calories is practically unchanged.[12] As might be expected, the higher income elasticity implies lower levels of consumption for the lowest income groups and higher levels of consumption for people with higher incomes.

12. Notice that such a group could be defined as the deficitarian population if calorie requirement were to be 250 calories a day lower than the ones used through our exercise.

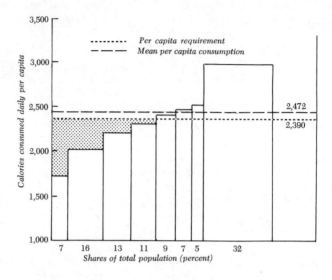

Figure 1. Calorie Consumption by Income Groups, Latin America, 1965, with Calorie-Income Elasticity Equal to 0.15

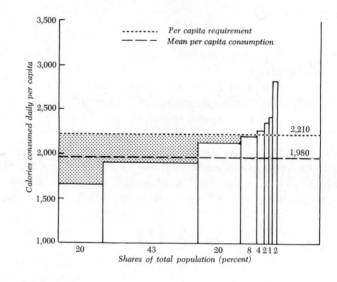

Figure 2. Calorie Consumption by Income Groups, Asia, 1965, with Calorie-Income Elasticity Equal to 0.15

Figure 3. Calorie Consumption by Income Groups, Middle East, 1965,
with Calorie-Income Elasticity Equal to 0.15

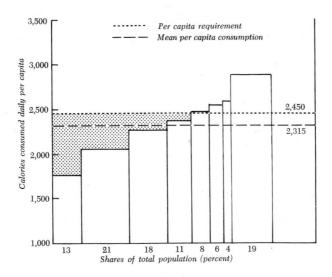

Figure 4. Calorie Consumption by Income Groups, Africa, 1965,
with Calorie-Income Elasticity Equal to 0.15

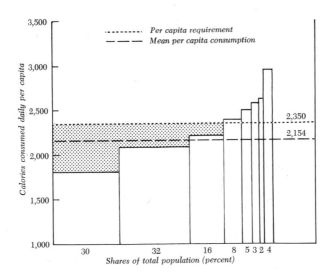

Figure 5. Calorie Consumption by Income Groups, Latin America, 1965, with Calorie-Income Elasticity Equal to 0.30

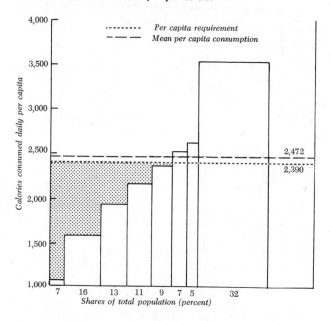

Figure 6. Calorie Consumption by Income Groups, Asia, 1965, with Calorie-Income Elasticity Equal to 0.30

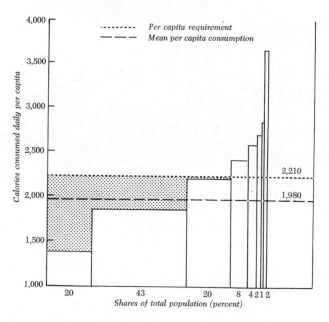

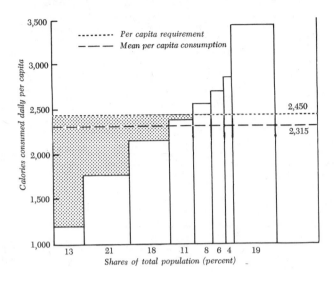

Figure 7. Calorie Consumption by Income Groups, Middle East, 1965, with Calorie-Income Elasticity Equal to 0.30

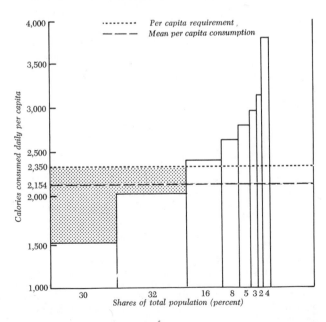

Figure 8. Calorie Consumption by Income Groups, Africa, with Calorie-Income Elasticity Equal to 0.30

Table 8. Number of People Consuming Insufficient Calories, and Calorie Deficits in Developing Countries, by Regions, 1965

Region	Population with daily calorie deficits				Total daily calorie deficit (thousand millions)
	More than 250 calories		Fewer than 250 calories		
	Millions of people	Average deficit	Millions of people	Average deficit	
Calorie income elasticity: 0.15					
Latin America	55	450	58	131	32
Asia	563	364	173	116	225
Middle East	75	407	16	94	32
Africa	151	380	39	72	61
Total	844		286		350
Calorie income elasticity: 0.30					
Latin America	87	783	26	211	74
Asia	563	503	0	0	283
Middle East	48	906	25	60	45
Africa	151	570	0	0	86
Total	849		51		488

This means higher deficits for the lowest income groups but elimination of deficits for higher income groups. The net effect is a larger total calories deficit.

Table 9 presents comparisons of the total daily calorie deficit estimated on the basis of average consumption levels by income groups with earlier estimates based on country or regional average levels of consumption.[13] Estimates based on regional averages are too low because they imply unrealistically that surplus consumption in some countries compensates for the deficits in other countries. Similarly, when the total deficit is calculated on the basis of country averages, surplus consumption by the higher income groups is assumed to compensate for the deficits in the low-income groups.

13. Estimates of the calorie deficit from regional averages (D^r) and country averages (D^c) were made on the basis of country data presented in Appendix A, as follows:

$$D^r = N(C^r - \Sigma(n_j/N)C_j^o) \text{ and}$$
$$D^c = N_1(C^r - \Sigma(n_k/N_1)C_k),$$

where C^r is per capita calorie requirement, n_j and C_j^o are, respectively, the population and per capita calorie consumption in each country of the region, and n_k and C_k^o are, respectively, the population and per capita calorie consumption in each country with a calorie deficit. N is the total population of the region, and N_1 is the population in all countries of the region with a per capita calorie deficit. See also Table D.2.

Table 9. Estimates of Total Daily Calorie Deficits in Developing
Countries, 1965, Based on Regional, Country, and Income Group
Averages
(Thousand millions of calories)

			Income group averages	
Region	Regional averages	Country averages	Elasticity =0.15	Elasticity =0.30
Latin America	0	19	32	74
Asia	202	213	225	283
Middle East	19	32	32	45
Africa	48	50	61	86
Total	269	314	350	488

Sources: Regional averages, computed by multiplying the region's population by the mean per capita deficit—the difference between per capita requirements and the mean per capita consumption—of the region; country averages, computed by adding each country's deficit, which is obtained by multiplying its population by the difference between per capita requirements and the per capita consumption of the country.

At this point a few thoughts and figures may help to put into some perspective the magnitudes discussed so far. The estimated daily deficit of 350 thousand million calories amounted to approximately 11 percent of total calorie consumption in the developing countries and to approximately 4 percent of worldwide calorie consumption in 1965. An estimated daily deficit of 350 thousand million calories is equivalent to approximately 100,000 metric tons of cereals.[14] On an annual basis, this deficit is equivalent to 36.5 million metric tons, equal to 3.8 percent of the world production of cereals and to 16.9 percent of cereal consumption in developing countries. The cost of this calorie deficit is approximately $7 thousand million, or 2.4 percent of total GNP in the developing countries and 0.3 percent of worldwide GNP in 1965. The calorie deficit in relation to regional magnitudes is shown in Table 10.

Providing for additional food and resources on these orders of magnitude would have constituted no small order. In reality, much larger quantities of food would have been needed, for it is hard to conceive of a program that would eliminate the deficit in the affected population without also increasing food consumption of the population already consuming an adequate supply of calories. The full cost of eliminating calorie deficits can be severalfold the cost of the food needed in target-group–oriented programs (see Chapter 4).

14. It is assumed that one metric ton of cereals has 3.5 million calories.

Table 10. Calorie Deficit in Relation to Regional Consumption and GNP, 1965

Region	Calorie deficit as a percentage of		Cost of calorie deficit as a percentage of GNP [b]
	Total calorie consumption	Total cereal consumption [a]	
Latin America	5	12	0.5
Asia	13	18	4.2
Middle East	10	13	1.6
Africa	11	19	3.9

a. Annual cereal consumption is 28, 128, 26, and 33 million metric tons in, respectively, Latin America, Asia, the Middle East, and Africa. (FAO, *Agricultural Commodity Projections, 1970–1980* [Rome, 1971].)

b. This cost estimate assumes that the calorie deficit would be made up by cereals at a retail cost of $200 a metric ton.

PROJECTIONS

The consumption functions developed on the basis of the 1965 data can be used to project the number of people consuming insufficient calories and the total calorie deficit in a later period. These projections are made with the assumption of alternative growth rates of per capita income and per capita calorie consumption, but no change in income distribution. It is assumed further that the shares of the population in each income group will remain as in 1965, while the absolute number of people and per capita income in each income group will grow at the same rate as in the total population. The population projections by income groups in each region are given in Table D.1 in Appendix D.

Per capita calorie consumption at any year T ($T=0$ is the base year) may be conveniently represented by equation (7):

(7) $C_T = (a + b \mathrm{Ln} X_T) e^{\lambda T}.$

Letting $X_T = X_o e^{\phi T}$, equation (7) becomes:

(8) $C_T = (a + b \mathrm{Ln}\, X_o + b\phi T) e^{\lambda T}$ or

(9) $C_T = (C_o + b\phi T) e^{\lambda T},$

where C_o is per capita consumption in the base period, ϕ is the growth rate of per capita income, and λ is the growth rate in consumption as a result of factors other than the growth in per capita income. $\lambda = 0$ implies that per capita calorie supply increases just enough to meet the demand generated by the growth in per capita income. $\lambda \neq 0$ implies variation over time in demand or supply conditions. Greater awareness of the importance of good nutrition may be operative on the demand side. Most important, however, is the

Table 11. Annual Percentage Growth Rates of per Capita Income (ϕ) and Calorie Consumption from Other Sources (λ) Used in Three Projection Alternatives (A, B, and C)

	Alternatives					
	A		B		C	
Region	ϕ	λ	ϕ	λ	ϕ	λ
Latin America	2.0	0	3.0	0	3.0	0.25
Asia	1.0	0	2.0	0	2.0	0.25
Middle East	3.0	0	6.0	0	6.0	0.25
Africa	1.0	0	2.0	0	2.0	0.25

fact that consumption growth for any given level of income is likely to be the consequence of accelerated food production and reduction in the relative price of food.

In Table 11 the annual growth rates are given of per capita income (ϕ) and per capita calorie consumption as the result of factors other than income (λ) in three alternative projections of calorie deficits for the years 1975 and 1990.[15] Throughout the "Projections" section, the consumption level of each income group in 1965 is assumed to correspond with the values estimated on the basis of the lower income elasticity: that is, 0.15 at the level of the region's requirements. The estimated calorie consumption by income groups derived on the basis of equation (9) and the parameter estimates presented in Table 11 are given in Table 12.

The implied growth rates in the regions' overall calorie consumption for the three alternative projections are shown in Table 13. The three alternative projections bracket the growth rates that might realistically be expected to occur. The annual growth rate of per capita food production in the developing market economies has been estimated at 0.2 percent during 1962–72 and at 0.7 percent during the prior decade. For 1975 a realistic assessment would therefore be most appropriately consistent with projection alternative A. To achieve calorie consumption on the levels projected under alternative C, extraordinary efforts and success in expanding food production would be required, particularly because it is doubtful that per capita income will grow at the higher rate.

15. In calculating calorie consumption levels for 1975 and 1990 by equation (9), instantaneous annual growth was assumed. The consumption levels would have been slightly less had they been estimated on the assumption of discrete annual growth rates; alternatively, these estimates imply slightly higher annual growth rates than those given in Table 11.

Table 12. Projected Per Capita Calorie Consumption by Income
Groups, 1975 and 1990

Income group by region	1965	Alternative growth paths					
		A		B		C	
		1975	1990	1975	1990	1975	1990
Latin America							
I	1,747	1,819	1,927	1,855	2,016	1,901	2,145
II	2,021	2,093	2,201	2,129	2,290	2,182	2,437
III	2,204	2,276	2,384	2,312	2,473	2,370	2,631
IV	2,325	2,397	2,505	2,433	2,594	2,494	2,760
V	2,415	2,487	2,595	2,523	2,684	2,586	2,856
VI	2,487	2,559	2,667	2,595	2,756	2,660	2,932
VII	2,547	2,619	2,727	2,655	2,816	2,721	2,996
VIII	2,995	3,067	3,175	3,103	3,264	3,181	3,473
Mean	2,472	2,544	2,652	2,581	2,741	2,644	2,917
Asia							
I	1,671	1,704	1,754	1,737	1,837	1,781	1,955
II	1,924	1,957	2,007	1,990	2,090	2,040	2,224
III	2,094	2,127	2,177	2,160	2,260	2,214	2,405
IV	2,206	2,239	2,289	2,272	2,372	2,329	2,524
V	2,289	2,322	2,372	2,355	2,455	2,414	2,612
VI	2,356	2,389	2,439	2,422	2,522	2,483	2,683
VII	2,411	2,444	2,494	2,477	2,577	2,539	2,742
VIII	2,822	2,855	2,905	2,888	2,988	2,960	3,179
Mean	1,980	2,013	2,063	2,446	2,146	2,097	2,283
Middle East							
I	1,763	1,873	2,039	1,983	2,315	2,033	2,463
II	2,044	2,154	2,320	2,264	2,596	2,321	2,762
III	2,232	2,342	2,508	2,452	2,784	2,513	2,962
IV	2,356	2,466	2,632	2,576	2,908	2,640	3,094
V	2,448	2,558	2,724	2,668	3,000	2,735	3,192
VI	2,522	2,632	2,798	2,742	3,074	2,811	3,271
VII	2,583	2,693	2,859	2,803	3,135	2,873	3,336
VIII	2,875	2,983	3,151	3,095	3,427	3,172	3,646
Mean	2,315	2,426	2,592	2,536	2,868	2,599	3,051
Africa							
I	1,829	1,864	1,917	1,899	1,995	1,946	2,123
II	2,098	2,133	2,186	2,168	2,264	2,222	2,409
III	2,278	2,313	2,366	2,348	2,444	2,407	2,600
IV	2,397	2,432	2,485	2,467	2,563	2,529	2,727
V	2,486	2,521	2,574	2,556	2,652	2,620	2,822
VI	2,557	2,592	2,645	2,627	2,723	2,693	2,897
VII	2,616	2,651	2,704	2,686	2,782	2,753	2,960
VIII	2,978	3,013	3,066	3,048	3,144	3,124	3,345
Mean	2,154	2,189	2,242	2,244	2,320	2,279	2,468

Table 13. Implied (Compounded) Annual Percentage Growth
Rates in Mean Regional per Capita Calorie Consumption,
Projections A, B, and C

Region	Growth rates (percent)		
	A	B	C
Latin America	0.3	0.4	0.7
Asia	0.2	0.3	0.6
Middle East	0.5	0.9	1.1
Africa	0.2	0.3	0.5

The daily per capita calorie deficit estimates in the affected population groups by 1975 and 1990 are given in Table D.3 in Appendix D. The estimated size of the undernourished population in 1975 and 1990 under the alternative projections is shown in Table 14 and Figure 9. The total calorie deficits are estimated under the three alternative projection assumptions and are shown in Table 15.

The above projections warrant several conclusions. Per capita growth in food consumption that is just sufficient to meet the demand generated by the growth in per capita income, without income redistribution, would make little contribution to the reduction of calorie undernutrition. By contrast, high rates of growth in per capita food consumption (based on high rates of food availability and lower food prices) could substantially reduce undernutrition by 1990, provided that income and food consumption in the lowest income groups grow at the same rate as in the higher income groups. Under projection Alternative C, the proportion of the severely undernourished (in excess of 250 calories below requirements) in the total population could be expected to decline from 55 percent in 1965 to 12 percent by 1990.

Given realistic assumptions, however, about per capita income growth rates and possibilities for accelerating food production at prevailing production costs, we believe that only government intervention specifically designed to subsidize food production or to assist the poor to achieve minimally satisfactory levels of food consumption could lead to the elimination of undernutrition. Various program options directed to this goal are discussed in the final chapter.

DEFICITS BY AGE GROUPS: INFANT MALNUTRITION

Average per capita nutrition data do not address the problem of the distribution of nutrition intake within the family. Although per

Table 14. Size of Undernourished Population, 1975 and 1990, with Alternative Projections
(Population in millions)

Region	Population with calorie deficits below requirements			Population with calorie deficit in excess of 250 calories below requirements		
	A	B	C	A	B	C
1975						
Latin America	112 (0.36) [a]	112 (0.36)	112 (0.36)	71 (0.23)	71 (0.23)	21 (0.07)
Asia	924 (0.82)	924 (0.82)	707 (0.63)	707 (0.63)	707 (0.63)	221 (0.20)
Middle East	94 (0.51)	61 (0.33)	61 (0.33)	61 (0.33)	24 (0.13)	24 (0.13)
Africa	243 (0.77)	193 (0.61)	193 (0.61)	93 (0.61)	93 (0.61)	93 (0.61)
Total	1,373 (0.71)	1,290 (0.66)	1,073 (0.55)	932 (0.48)	895 (0.42)	359 (0.19)
1990						
Latin America	102 (0.23)	102 (0.23)	30 (0.07)	30 (0.07)	30 (0.07)	30 (0.07)
Asia	1,299 (0.82)	994 (0.63)	994 (0.63)	311 (0.20)	311 (0.20)	311 (0.20)
Middle East	89 (0.34)	35 (0.13)	0	35 (0.13)	0	0
Africa	280 (0.62)	280 (0.62)	135 (0.30)	135 (0.30)	135 (0.30)	0
Total	1,770 (0.64)	1,411 (0.51)	1,159 (0.42)	511 (0.19)	476 (0.17)	341 (0.12)

a. Figures in parentheses represent percentage of total population.

Figure 9. Estimated Undernourished Population and Total Population, 1965, and Three Alternative Projections, 1975 and 1990

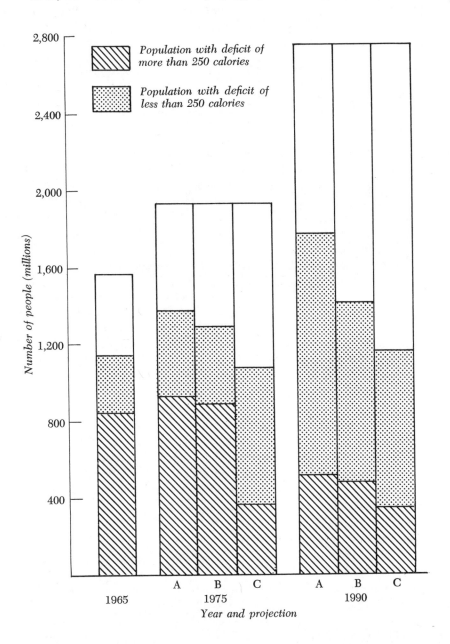

**Table 15. Daily Calorie Deficit, 1975 and 1990,
with Alternative Projections**
(Thousand millions of calories)

Region	1975			1990		
	A	B	C	A	B	C
Latin America	32	27	21	27	18	7
Asia	283	253	222	291	198	79
Middle East	28	18	15	21	5	—
Africa	69	60	50	82	60	31
Total	412	358	308	421	281	117

capita figures might well show an intake above requirements, some family members—particularly classified by age groups—experience a strong deficit of that particular nutrient. Protein-calorie deficiency in infants and young children appears to be one of the main features of the overall nutrition problem in developing countries. The magnitude of the problem appears not only in its rate of incidence in low-income families of these countries but also in its potential effect on the physical and mental development of the individual.

In an attempt to evaluate the effect of income on the nutrient intake by age groups, it is useful to review data for Calcutta and to examine some of the evidence on the decline in breastfeeding, one of the principal factors in infant undernutrition in urban areas of developing countries.

Data on the intake of nutrients by age groups are extremely difficult and expensive to generate, and few studies report on such data out of food surveys. Perhaps the best source of such data, and worth examining as an illustrative case, is the Calcutta Food Survey undertaken in 1969.[16]

A summary is given of the mean intake of different nutrients (as a percentage of the requirements) by selected age groups for the poorest one-third of the families in Calcutta (see Table 16). They correspond to all families with a monthly per capita expenditure of less than 40 rupees a month. A strong difference is evident between the deficit in calories and in proteins; although protein consumption is relatively close to requirements, the deficit in calories is substantial for all age groups.

The implications of such a calorie deficit, particularly for young children, are of prime importance. When the body lacks calories, it uses up protein as a source of energy. Proteins, therefore, are not

16. U.S., Agency for International Development, *Food Habits in Calcutta.*

Table 16. Mean Intake of Nutrients in the Poorest One-Third of Calcutta Families, by Age Groups
(Percentage of requirements)

Age group	Calories	Proteins	Calcium	Vitamin A
2–4 years	55	105	70	75
12–16 years	56	85	69	65
22–56 years	59	95	94	69

Source: U.S., Agency for International Development, *A Study of Food Habits in Calcutta* (Calcutta: Hindustan Thompson Associates, 1972).

available for other uses such as cell maintenance and cell formation.

To determine the effect of income on nutrition, the intake of each nutrient by age group was regressed on the per capita expenditure of the family. The results are given in Table 17, where β represents the expenditure elasticity of the nutrient in question.

The regression results do not appear significant for iron except for children younger than one year. For all other nutrients the results are highly significant except for infants younger than six months. There are three principal results.

First, all elasticities are smaller than 1 and most are smaller than one-half; this is simply Engel's law. Although expressions allowing for a variable elasticity were attempted, the constant elasticity form gave the best fit.

Second, it is possible to observe certain patterns of the elasticity across age groups. Young children appear to have a higher elasticity than older children and adults. Therefore, although nutrition intake does not grow at an equal rate with income, there is a positive redistribution toward young children.

Third, the elasticities for calories and proteins are extremely close, suggesting that both are derived from the same staple. With increased income, consumption of that staple is simply increased without major shifts toward other types of foods.

Finally, because the survey provides data on the fraction of vegetarians in each expenditure bracket, that information is included as an additional explanatory variable (see Table 18).

Results of Table 18 show that the fraction-of-vegetarians variable is significant in explaining nutritional intakes of infants younger than six months; in addition, it increases substantially the coefficient and significance of the expenditure variable. Holding constant food habits as determined by vegetarian practices, the effect of income on infant nutrition becomes quite strong.

The coefficient of the fraction-of-vegetarians variable is negative: that is, when income is held constant, vegetarian habits have a

Table 17. Expenditure Elasticities (β) of Different Nutrients, by Age Groups and Sex, Calcutta

Age	Calories β	Calories R^2 [a]	Protein β	Protein R^2 [a]	Vitamin A β	Vitamin A R^2 [a]	Iron β	Iron R^2 [a]	Calcium β	Calcium R^2 [a]
Younger than 6 months	0.44 (1.68)	0.19	0.44 (1.42)	0.11	0.18 (0.31)	0	0.57 (3.65)	0.61	0.49 (1.87)	0.24
Younger than 1 year	0.26 (3.03)	0.43	0.33 (4.17)	0.60	0.55 (7.24)	0.82	0.35 (3.19)	0.46	0.37 (3.42)	0.49
1–2 years	0.31 (13.66)	0.94	0.38 (11.89)	0.92	0.63 (7.21)	0.81	0.05 (1.73)	0.14	0.61 (11.13)	0.91
2–3 years	0.32 (10.64)	0.90	0.32 (8.59)	0.85	0.55 (8.58)	0.85	0.04 (0.38)	0	0.50 (8.06)	0.83
3–4 years	0.33 (14.84)	0.94	0.29 (12.94)	0.93	0.43 (7.86)	0.82	0.03 (0.65)	0	0.55 (10.01)	0.88
4–5 years	0.21 (5.30)	0.68	0.19 (5.31)	0.68	0.41 (6.54)	0.76	−0.08 (1.21)	0.04	0.59 (9.02)	0.86
5–6 years	0.26 (8.90)	0.86	0.24 (6.02)	0.73	0.39 (4.49)	0.60	0.06 (1.45)	0.08	0.56 (13.70)	0.94
7–11 years	0.24 (8.87)	0.86	0.19 (5.00)	0.65	0.39 (5.55)	0.70	0.05 (2.42)	0.27	0.39 (4.10)	0.55
12–16 years (male)	0.18 (8.40)	0.84	0.12 (2.72)	0.33	0.25 (4.10)	0.55	0.04 (1.12)	0.02	0.24 (2.43)	0.27
12–16 years (female)	0.24 (9.04)	0.86	0.24 (6.27)	0.75	0.34 (3.85)	0.52	0.05 (1.62)	0.11	0.46 (6.87)	0.78
17–21 years (male)	0.17 (8.51)	0.85	0.17 (5.30)	0.68	0.32 (4.11)	0.55	0.02 (0.52)	0	0.36 (9.27)	0.87
17–21 years (female)	0.16 (4.85)	0.63	0.14 (3.88)	0.52	0.14 (1.71)	0.13	−.001 (0.02)	0	0.35 (7.64)	0.82
22–56 years (male)	0.20 (15.16)	0.95	0.19 (14.17)	0.94	0.27 (3.84)	0.52	0.05 (3.80)	0.51	0.42 (13.91)	0.94
22–56 years (female)	0.20 (13.90)	0.94	0.17 (9.40)	0.87	0.34 (7.17)	0.80	−0.02 (1.06)	0.01	0.41 (13.80)	0.94
57 years+ (male)	0.23 (5.86)	0.72	0.23 (6.86)	0.78	0.30 (3.27)	0.43	0.08 (1.76)	0.14	0.48 (10.63)	0.90

Note: Figures in parentheses are t-statistics.
a. Coefficient of determination.

negative effect on the child's nutrition status. The earlier, low figure of the elasticity of expenditure was therefore probably a combination of the positive income effect and the negative vegetarian effect because a higher fraction of vegetarians was found in the higher income groups.

The analysis of the Calcutta data might be interpreted superficially to mean that income growth improves nutrition in all age groups. It must be noted, however, that the data pertained only to purchased food. The decline in breastfeeding practices is perhaps the most distinctive feature behind infant undernutrition in urban areas; urbanization tends to shorten the breastfeeding period. In evidence summarized by Berg for countries such as Guatemala, Indonesia, Taiwan, and Zambia, a strong difference in the fraction of mothers breastfeeding is found between urban and rural areas.[17] Jelliffe reviewed similar evidence for Jamaica, Brazil, Chile, Panama, and Guatemala.[18] Specific urban-rural comparisons for the poorer segments of the population in Jamaica and Guatemala show the same pattern; in the case of Guatemala, rural Indians breastfeed two and a half years, compared with less than half a year for low-income urban groups. Although among lower income mothers in Singapore in 1951, 62 percent of babies were breastfed at six months of age, the figure declined to 27 percent in 1960.

Of several determining factors in the decline in breastfeeding practices in low-income urban groups, some are sociological, such as imitation of other socioeconomic groups;[19] others are economic, perhaps the most important of which is the increased participation of women in the labor force.

Infant malnutrition as a result of absence from the home of lactating mothers participating in the labor force is an interesting case of income redistribution within the family in the face of urbanization: although the family's real monetary income rises because of the mother's work, the child suffers a "negative income effect." Unless sufficient food for the infant to compensate for nutrients lost by reduced breastfeeding is provided from that increased family income, that negative income effect remains.[20] This will basically depend on the marginal propensity to spend on food for the infant.

A rough estimate has been made, for urban India, of the required marginal propensity to spend on the infant so as to maintain constant his nutritional status. Assume that the mother substitutes commercially sold cow milk (M_c), purchased at price (P_c), for

17. Alan Berg, *The Nutrition Factor: Its Role in National Development* (Cambridge, Mass.: M.I.T. Press, 1973).

18. D. Jelliffe, *Infant Nutrition in the Subtropics and Tropics* (Geneva: World Health Organization, 1955).

19. Ibid.

20. Breastfeeding provides other benefits: for example, it extends the spacing of births and diminishes exposure of the infant to health hazards in unsanitary environments.

Table 18. Expenditure and Fraction-of-Vegetarians' Elasticities Obtained by Multiple Regressions

Age group	Calories			Proteins			Vitamin A		
	Expenditure	Vegetarians	$R^{2\,a}$	Expenditure	Vegetarians	$R^{2\,a}$	Expenditure	Vegetarians	$R^{2\,a}$
Younger than 0.5 year	1.12 (3.71)	-11.85 (2.85)	0.70	1.28 (3.97)	-14.68 (3.31)	0.73	1.73 (2.83)	-72.20 (3.22)	0.64
0.5–1 year							0.24 (3.34)	0.49 [a] (5.00)	0.96
4–5 years							0.22 (3.24)	0.37 (3.41)	0.89
22–56 years	0.22 (15.42)	0.80 (2.62)	0.97						

Note: Figures in parentheses are *t*-statistics.
a. Indicates the coefficient of the vegetarian variable in its natural form.

a fraction of breast milk (M_B). When she goes to work and earns an income (ΔY), the required marginal propensity can be calculated by the expression:

$$m = \frac{P_c \cdot \alpha \cdot M_B}{\Delta Y},$$

where α represents a conversion factor between both types of milk to correct for different nutrient contents.[21]

In calculating the value of m, it was assumed that because the mother goes to work the infant receives only 30 percent of her potential breast milk: that is, the required marginal propensity out of the increased income of the family to spend on the infant's milk must be sufficiently high to substitute for the loss of 70 percent of the mother's breast milk. The monthly cost of replacing 70 percent of breast milk at different ages of the infant is shown in row 4, Table 19. The comparison of such figures with a rough estimate of the monthly income of an unskilled woman in urban India gives the implicit required marginal propensity to spend in commercial milk for the child's purpose. It amounts to 0.53 in the first six months of the infant's life (see row 6, Table 19).

The figure of 0.53 may be compared with the marginal propensity

---

21. The amount of cow milk required is $M_c = \alpha \cdot M_B$. The equivalent marginal propensity times the income change equals the expenditure on milk: that is, $m \cdot \Delta Y = P_c \cdot M_c$. Combining the two equations yields the expression in the text.

Table 19. Required Marginal Propensity to Spend on Milk to Maintain Nutritional Status of Children, Calcutta

Item	\multicolumn{5}{c}{Infants' ages (months)}				
	0–6	*7–12*	*13–18*	*19–24*	*0–24*
1. Monthly potential breast milk (liters)	25.9	15.2	15.2	6.1	15.6
2. Cow milk equivalent (liters)	30.5	17.5	17.5	7.0	18.2
3. Cost of milk equivalent (rupees)	91.5	52.5	52.5	21.0	54.6
4. 70 percent of row 3, above	64.0	36.7	36.7	14.7	38.2
5. Monthly income of unskilled woman, 1973 (rupees)	120	120	120	120	120
6. Required marginal propensity to spend on milk	0.53	0.30	0.30	0.12	0.32

Sources: rows 1 and 2, Alan Berg, *The Nutrition Factor: Its Role in National Development* (Cambridge, Mass.: M.I.T. Press, 1973); row 3, using a price of 3 rupees a liter (price as of October 1972 in Bombay and Madras); row 5, corresponds approximately to the monthly wage of a woman in domestic service in a large urban area.

to spend on food observed in the Calcutta Food Survey. That observed value, for children of younger than one year, is below 0.06, almost one-tenth of the required value. This strong difference between the observed and required marginal propensity gives support to the conclusion that, even under optimistic assumptions, a decline in breastfeeding as a result of the mother's participation in the labor force could have an important negative effect on the nutritional status of the child.

3

Cost Effectiveness of
Some Policy Options

EVALUATION OF POLICY OPTIONS directed toward increasing the nutritional intake of a target group would require answers to the following questions: (a) What are the variables explaining the behavior of the typical low-income urban household in relation to its intake (and distribution within the household) of different nutrients? Such variables would be both economic—that is, income and the relative cost of different nutrients—as well as cultural determinants of food habits. (b) Which of these variables can be affected by policy instruments in the short and long run? (c) What is the cost effectiveness of inducing changes in different variables: that is, the cost incurred by that policy per unit change in nutrient consumption by the target group?

This study does not address this full set of questions; rather, it concentrates basically on (c), the cost effectiveness of alternative policies. For such a discussion it is useful to distinguish between two large typologies of policies (and programs): "countrywide" and "target-group oriented." The former includes those programs which reach the target group in the process of reaching all segments of the population. Given that these programs require a subsidy or transfer payment, nontarget groups also get subsidized. Target-oriented programs, on the other hand, are those in which particular target groups (by income categories, by age groups, and so forth) may be reached without subsidizing nontarget groups.

Most of the policy options discussed here are applicable only to urban populations because many of the target-oriented programs are almost impossible to institutionalize in a rural environment. This makes the discussion easier inasmuch as there is no need to trace the nutrition impact of income effects derived from changes in rural production and incomes, as induced by alternative food policies.

In the first section below the cost effectiveness of a general (urban) food price subsidy is examined. The modifications needed to analyze the cost effectiveness of a policy that aims at nutrient-specific objectives is described in the second section. In Chapter 4 the cost effectiveness of target-group–oriented programs is considered, specifically a food price subsidy, an income transfer, and a food stamp program.

A General (Urban) Food Price Subsidy

Assume two groups of urban consumers of a particular food commodity: the target, or poorer, group (group p) and the remaining, or richer, consumers (group r). We begin by defining:

$$(10) \qquad\qquad \eta_T = \alpha\,\eta_p + (1-\alpha)\eta_r,$$

where η_T is the (absolute) price elasticity of the demand for the commodity expressed as the weighted average of the elasticities of both groups; and α represents the share of consumption of the poorer group. The object is to increase the consumption of this food in the target group by a fraction equal to λ by reducing the price to consumers through a price subsidy. If the initial price is equal to 1, two equations result:

(11) *Target* $\qquad\qquad \lambda = \eta_p dp^d$ and

(12) *Aggregate equilibrium* $\quad \eta_T dp^d = \epsilon dp^s,$

where dp^d and dp^s are the percentage changes in the demand and supply prices, and where ϵ represents the price elasticity of supply. Solving for dp^d and dp^s gives:

$$(13) \qquad\qquad dp^d = \frac{\lambda}{\eta_p} \text{ and}$$

$$(14) \qquad\qquad dp^s = \left(\frac{\eta_T}{\eta_p}\right)\left(\frac{\lambda}{\epsilon}\right).$$

Denoting S the fiscal cost of the subsidy as a fraction of the initial (urban) expenditure in the commodity, it is possible to write:

$$(15) \qquad S = (dp^d + dp^s)(1 + \eta_T\,dp^d) \text{ and}$$

$$(16) \qquad S = \frac{\lambda}{\eta_p}\left(1 + \frac{\eta_T}{\epsilon}\right)\left(1 + \lambda\frac{\eta_T}{\eta_p}\right).$$

Equation (16), when evaluated for a situation where the commodity is partly imported ($\epsilon = \infty$), must be interpreted as the cost of a general consumption subsidy that does not discriminate between imports and domestic production. Domestic producers continue to receive the world price of the commodity.

An alternative, quite common policy is to subsidize only the imported fraction of the commodity. Although this policy reduces the fiscal cost, it also induces a fall in farm income and a production efficiency loss because imports replace cheaper domestic production. Under such a policy the value of S becomes:

$$(17) \qquad S = \frac{\lambda}{\eta_p}\left[\left(1 + \lambda\,\frac{\eta_T}{\eta_p}\right) - \pi\left(1 - \lambda\,\frac{\epsilon}{\eta_p}\right)\right],$$

where π is the initial fraction of domestic production in total consumption, and ϵ represents the domestic supply elasticity. Correspondingly, the efficiency loss of the policy, expressed as a fraction of the initial expenditure on the commodity, may be written as:[1]

$$(18) \qquad L = \tfrac{1}{2}\left(\frac{\lambda}{\eta_p}\right)^2 \pi\,\epsilon.$$

An expression of the cost effectiveness of this policy, the cost per additional unit of food consumed by the target group as a ratio of the food's preprogram price, may be written as:

$$(19) \qquad s = \left(\frac{S}{\lambda\alpha}\right).$$

---

1. The efficiency loss is derived by assuming a linear supply function of domestic producers. It is of interest to compare the tradeoff between the fiscal gain and the (production) efficiency loss in using this alternative policy. The fiscal gain is the difference between equation (16), evaluated with $\epsilon = \infty$, and equation (17) where ϵ must be interpreted as the elasticity of domestic supply:

(1′)   Fiscal gain = $FG = \dfrac{\lambda}{\eta_p}\left(1 + \lambda\dfrac{\eta_T}{\eta_p}\right) - \dfrac{\lambda}{\eta_p}\left[\left(1 + \lambda\dfrac{\eta_T}{\eta_p}\right) - \pi\left(1 - \lambda\dfrac{\epsilon}{\eta_p}\right)\right]$, or

(2′) $FG = \pi\dfrac{\lambda}{\eta_p}\left(1 - \lambda\dfrac{\epsilon}{\eta_p}\right)$.

The fiscal gain will be larger than the efficiency loss, $FG > L$, when:

(3′) $\left(1 - \lambda\dfrac{\epsilon}{\eta_p}\right) > \tfrac{1}{2}\lambda\dfrac{\epsilon}{\eta_p}$, or

(4′) $\lambda\dfrac{\epsilon}{\eta_p} < (\tfrac{2}{3})$.

The fiscal gain will be greater as long as $\left(\lambda\dfrac{\epsilon}{\eta_p}\right)$ is less than two-thirds.

Table 20. Cost Effectiveness and Efficiency Loss of a Food Price Subsidy, Expressed as a Ratio of the Price per Unit

Program		$\alpha=0.2$		$\alpha=0.7$	
		$\eta_p=0.5$	$\eta_p=1.0$	$\eta_p=0.5$	$\eta_p=1.0$
General consumption subsidy	$\epsilon=1.0$	18.0	8.9	5.1	3.1
	$\epsilon=\infty$	12.0	5.6	3.4	1.7
Subsidy on imports	$\pi=0.25$	10.5 (0.5)	4.6 (0.13)	3.0 (0.14)	1.4 (0.04)
	$\pi=0.50$	9.0 (1.0)	3.6 (0.25)	2.6 (0.28)	1.1 (0.07)
	$\pi=0.75$	7.5 (1.5)	2.6 (0.38)	2.1 (0.43)	0.8 (0.11)

Note: $\lambda = 0.2$; $\eta_r = 0.5$. Figures in parentheses show the efficiency loss $(L/\lambda\alpha)$.

Equation (19) presents the value of s in terms of the initial price of the commodity, which has the role of a scaling factor.[2]

The values of s for selected parameters are given in Table 20. It would appear at first that any program in which the cost of delivering a unit of food exceeds the unit price of that food cannot be very cost effective. Yet, as will be shown later, the cost of delivering a unit of additional food directly to the target population will usually also be in excess of the unit price of the food. Both in theory and by hard evidence it has been found impossible to fine-tune food assistance programs so that every additional unit of food delivered is converted into a full additional unit of food consumed. Furthermore, direct food assistance programs usually entail high delivery costs in addition to the cost of the food itself.

Clearly, when the target population, and hence its share in the total consumption of a given food (α) is small, the fiscal cost of a general subsidy program per added unit of consumption in the target group becomes prohibitively expensive. The application of such a program would be least desirable in a middle-income country with a large share of the population already receiving adequate nutrition and an inelastic food supply. On the contrary, general food subsidy programs might be very cost-effective alternatives to target-group–oriented programs in countries where a large proportion of the population is inadequately fed (α is high) and the food supply relatively elastic.

2. Accordingly, the efficiency loss per extra unit of food consumed by the target groups may be defined as $L/\lambda\alpha$.

The higher fiscal cost effectiveness of a general food subsidy program in a poor country (with a high α) unfortunately does not suggest that such a country is in a better position to eliminate nutritional deficiencies than the richer country (with a low α). In equation (16) it can be seen that the total cost is the same for both types of countries (independent of the value of α) when $\eta_p = \eta_r = \eta_T$. With a demand elasticity of 0.5, the cost is about equal to the country's urban expenditure on that food if the supply elasticity is 0.5 and about half that cost if food supply is infinitely elastic. The cost, however, will be a much higher proportion of GNP for the poorer country and therefore a much greater budgetary burden.

To illustrate the point, the total cost of such programs for a particular food commodity, cereals, has been computed. In Table 21 this cost is presented as a fraction of the GNP of the country, for alternative values of per capita income of the country and the world price of cereals. In these calculations the urban population is assumed to represent half of the total population. The figures in Table 21 suggest that for a country such as India, with a per capita income of $100, the total cost of such a program becomes prohibitively expensive under existing world prices of cereals.

It may be concluded, therefore, that the total cost of the program relative to GNP is not an argument extraneous to the choice of a cost-effective program. Our original observation that a general

Table 21. Fiscal Cost and Efficiency Loss of Alternative Price Subsidy Policies for Cereals, as a Percentage of GNP

Program	Per capita income of the country (U.S. dollars)	Cost of policy at different per ton world prices of cereals (percent of GNP)	
		US$200	US$300
General consumption subsidy ($\epsilon = \infty$)	100	5.6	8.3
	300	1.9	2.8
Subsidy on imports ($\epsilon = 1$; $\pi = 0.5$)	100	3.8 (0.3)	5.7 (0.5)
	300	1.3 (0.1)	1.9 (0.2)

Note: $\lambda = \alpha = 0.2$; $\eta_r = 0.5$; $\eta_p = 0.75$. The values in parentheses refer to the efficiency loss. The following expressions are used to compute the figures in the table:

Fiscal cost	$(p/y)l_u \cdot q_u \cdot S$ and
Efficiency loss	$(p/y)l_u \cdot q_u \cdot L$,

where (p/y) is the ratio of the world price of cereals with respect to the per capita income of the country, l_u is the share of urban population, and q_u is the yearly per capita physical consumption of cereals in urban areas. l_u was assumed to be 0.5 and $q_u = 0.182$ metric tons a year, equivalent to 500 grams a day.

food subsidy program is more cost effective in a poor country may need modification if such a country cannot bear the cost. Regardless of a high level of food deficiency affecting a large part of the population, the country may be forced to scale down its program objectives: the percentage of additional food to be given (λ) and the share of the population with the most severe deficiencies to be reached (α). In that case such a country would also have to resort to more cost-effective target-group–oriented programs to reduce undernutrition among the worst affected of the population.

FOOD SUBSIDIES AND THEIR EFFECTIVENESS
RELATIVE TO PARTICULAR NUTRIENTS

A rigorous comparison of the cost effectiveness of price subsidies on alternative foods ought to be carried out in relation to the particular nutrient in question (where calories may be considered a nutrient). The proper cost concept is the cost of an incremental unit of a nutrient (consumed by the target group) as a consequence of price subsidies on alternative food commodities. This becomes particularly important when the subsidy on a particular food, because of cross effects in consumption, changes the amount of other food commodities consumed.

The new concept introduced here is the elasticity of nutrient N with respect to the price of food 1: that is, the percentage increase in the intake of N when the price of that food commodity changes by 1 percent. Of obvious interest here is the elasticity relevant to the particular target group being analyzed.

Let us define such elasticity as E_{N1}:

$$(20) \qquad E_{N1} = n_1\,\eta_{11} + n_2\,\eta_{21} + n_3\,\eta_{31} \ldots n_M\,\eta_{M1},$$

where M represents the number of food commodities, and η_{11} and η_{i1} the own and cross-price elasticities with respect to the price of food 1 in the target group, respectively; and n_i represents the (base period) share of the total intake of nutrient N derived from consuming food i in the target group.

A price subsidy to food 1 will increase the intake of nutrient N only if E_{N1} is negative; such a result is not obvious and will depend on the sign of the η_{ij}s, namely, to what extent other food commodities are (gross) substitutes or complements of food commodity 1. If commodity 1 is a superior good, then η_{11} will always be negative;

in this case a negative value of E_{N1} is obtained under either of the following conditions described by equations (21) and (22):

$$(21) \qquad \sum_{i>1} n_i\, \eta_{i1} \leq 0,$$

that is, on the average, other food commodities are complements or, at most, unrelated to food commodity 1, where the n_is are the weights in computing such an average, or:

$$(22) \qquad \sum_{i>1} n\, \eta_{i1} > 0; \qquad \text{but} -\eta_{11} > \sum_{i>1} \frac{n_i}{n_1} \eta_{i1}.$$

On the average other food commodities are substitutes, but in absolute terms the weighted sum of their elasticities is lower than the own-price elasticity of food commodity 1.

With E_{N1} defined, the fiscal cost per unit increment in nutrient N may be computed in a way analogous to that in the preceding section. The only difference is that now λ is replaced by λ_N: that is, the objective is to increase the intake of nutrient N in the target group by a fraction equal to λ_N:

$$(23) \qquad \lambda_N = E_{N1}\, dp^d \text{ and}$$

$$(24) \qquad \eta_T\, dp^d = \epsilon dp^s.$$

Solving for dp^d and dp^s and substituting into equation (15), the following is obtained:

$$(25) \qquad S_N = \frac{\lambda_N}{E_{N1}}\left(1 + \frac{\eta_T}{\epsilon}\right)\left(1 + \lambda_N \frac{\eta_T}{E_{N1}}\right),$$

where S_N is the fiscal cost of the subsidy as a fraction of the initial total expenditure in commodity 1, aimed at achieving an increase in the intake of N in the target group by a fraction λ_N; and η_T is the (own-) price elasticity of demand for commodity 1 by all groups.

Equation (25) is quite symmetric with equation (16) developed earlier; λ has been replaced by λ_N and E_{N1}, or the nutrient elasticity, has been substituted for η_p.

The cost per unit increment in the intake of nutrient N may now be written:

$$(26) \qquad s_N = \left(\frac{n_1}{\alpha\, \lambda_N\, \phi_1}\right) S_N,$$

where ϕ_1 represents the amount of nutrient N per dollar spent in food commodity 1. α reflects again the (initial) share of such food consumed by the target group.

4

Programs Oriented to Target Groups

PROGRAMS THAT ARE ORIENTED TO TARGET GROUPS may range from straight income transfers and alleviation of unemployment to the delivery of specific foods to target groups. Possible program options include nutrition education, distribution of food at a price discount, food stamp programs for selected families, free food rations for selected families, food rations for children and pregnant mothers delivered to the home, and feeding of selected population groups in schools and factories.

The cost-effectiveness features of three target-group–oriented programs—a food price subsidy, a food stamp plan, and a straight income transfer—are considered here. A food price subsidy provides beneficiaries with as much food as they wish to purchase at a reduced price. A food stamp program, widely adopted in the United States, provides participants with the opportunity of purchasing a fixed amount of food at a lesser cost than market prices. These three options are examined by reference to a graphical analysis of a consumer's indifference curves in Figures 10 and 11.

The budget line X_oY_o in Figure 10 illustrates the opportunities a consumer has for allocating a fixed amount of income to food and nonfood purchases. Given the indifference curve AB, the initial equilibrium of the consumer is P, with an initial consumption of food equal to F. The curve OZ, the income-expenditure line, illustrates the consumer's preference for allocating increasing levels of income to food and nonfood purchases when the budget line has the same slope as X_oY_o: that is, the price ratio of food and nonfood remains constant.

46

**Figure 10. Analysis of the Cost
of a Food Stamp Program**

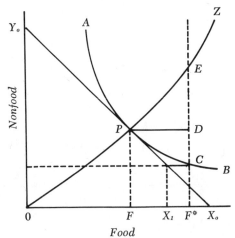

Food

The objective of the target-group–oriented program is to increase the consumer's food consumption from his initial level, *F*, to a higher level, *F**; we now consider the costs of alternative programs to reach this objective.

A FOOD STAMP PROGRAM

The cost of an optimal, as well as of a suboptimal, cost-effective food stamp program is illustrated in Figure 10. The optimal program would provide the consumer with a claim for food with a market value of *F** and charge him OX_1. The consumer will be in equilibrium at *C* and the cost of the program would be X_1F^*. Clearly, such a program would be highly cost effective; the beneficiary would spend not only the full income increment contained in the food subsidy, but would also transfer to food expenditure some of his own income formerly spent on other items.[1]

By reference to the cost effectiveness employed earlier, it is evident that the cost per unit of food reaching the target group would be less than the price of the food. To achieve such cost effectiveness, however, would require knowledge of the consumer's in-

---

1. Notice, however, that with this program the consumer is, at the margin, indifferent between participating or not participating in the food plan because his level of utility does not increase by participating in the program. In a rigorous definition, the optimal program is the one charging him the maximum price for the food coupon consistent with his participation in the program.

Figure 11. Analysis of the Cost of a Food Price Subsidy

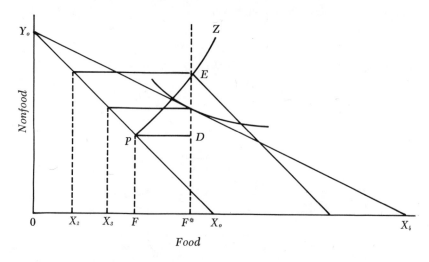

difference map (knowledge of point C). If, for example, consumer's preference for food is overestimated and he is charged OX_1, he may choose not to participate in the program.

A suboptimal but more realistic food stamp plan would set the cost of the food stamps at OF: that is, at the consumer's expenditure for food without the program. The consumer will be in equilibrium at D and the cost of such a suboptimal food plan becomes FF^*, the cost per unit of additional food consumed by the target group is just equal to the price of the food.

A basic condition for implementing a cost-effective food stamp program is differential costing of the stamps for participants in accord with their expenditures on food (and as a proxy of their income levels). Otherwise, those with the greatest need will refuse to participate in the program and participants who have higher-than-average incomes will use only a fraction of the subsidy for added food consumption.

INCOME TRANSFERS

Figure 11 shows that the income transfer required to induce a consumer to increase his food consumption from F to F^* is X_2F^*. What determines the cost effectiveness of an income transfer as a means of increasing food consumption is the slope of PZ; such a slope is determined by the marginal propensity to consume food in the relevant range of income changes induced by the transfer. Normally, the higher the income level of the target group, the lower the marginal propensity to consume food. Hence, an income transfer is relatively less cost effective. It is also noteworthy that the marginal propensity to consume food of desirable nutritional quality is usually lower in urban than in rural areas for a given food-nonfood price ratio and that the relative price of food is usually higher in urban areas. Consequently, income transfers are likely to be most cost ineffective for urban dwellers and for all but the poorest among them.

FOOD PRICE SUBSIDIES

A food price subsidy is illustrated in Figure 11 by the new budget line Y_oX_4. The cost of inducing food consumption to increase from F to F^* is equal to X_3F^*.

The extent of the price subsidy (that is, the required slope of the new budget line Y_oX_4) needed to induce food consumption at a level F^* depends on the curvature of the indifference map. Because it is safe to assume, however, that added food consumption has positive utility and the price elasticity for food is less than 1, the new price line must cross the F^* level of consumption between E and D[2]. This means that the cost of a food price subsidy, X_3F^*, will be less than the cost of a straight income transfer and more than the cost of a food stamp program.

SUMMARY OF COST-EFFECTIVENESS COMPARISONS

Cost-effectiveness formulas for the three target-group–oriented programs already described are summarized in Table 22. Such formulas define the cost of delivering an extra unit of food consumption as a fraction of the (preprogram) price of food. λ again represents the aimed increases in such consumption as a fraction of initial consumption.

The new parameters included in such formulas are m, or the marginal propensity to spend on food, and ϵ_p, the price elasticity of the (excess) supply faced by the target group. Such a supply

---

2. If the new price line crosses the F^* consumption level beneath point D, it means that the consumption of nonfood diminishes with the food price subsidy; that is, nonfood and food are gross substitutes. This can only be consistent with price elasticities for food larger than 1.

Table 22. Fiscal Cost of Supplying an Extra Unit of Food to the Target Group, Expressed as a Ratio of the Price per Unit

Program	$\epsilon_p = \infty$	$\epsilon_p < \infty$
Food stamp	1	$1 + \dfrac{1+\lambda}{\epsilon_p}$
Price subsidy	$\dfrac{1+\lambda}{\eta_p}$	$(1+\lambda)\left(\dfrac{1}{\epsilon_p} + \dfrac{1}{\eta_p}\right)$
Income transfer	$\dfrac{1}{m}$	$\dfrac{1}{m}\left[1 + (1+\lambda)\dfrac{\eta_p}{\epsilon_p}\right]$

is equal to the total supply of food minus the demand by the (richer) nontarget group; correspondingly, the price elasticity of such excess supply depends not only on the price elasticity of total supply, ϵ, but also on the price elasticity of demand of the nontarget group, η_R.[3]

When the programs have no effect on the supply price of food ($\epsilon_p = \infty$) some of the cost comparisons become rather straightforward. The least costly intervention is the suboptimal food stamp program described earlier, because the marginal propensity to spend in food as well as the price elasticity for food are bound to be less than 1;[4] the latter is particularly true if such programs are conceived for rather large aggregates of food commodities. Some illustrative estimates of the costs when the programs operate in an environment in which the additional food required raises the cost of food is provided in Table 23. The total supply elasticity has only a minor effect, contrary to what was observed earlier in reference to a general food price subsidy program. The explanation, of course, is that only relatively small quantities of additional food are needed in target-group–oriented programs. Consumption of the nontarget group not only does not increase, but even decreases, when total supply is not infinitely elastic.

For comparison, the cost of a general food price subsidy is shown in the last line of Table 23. These figures clearly illustrate that target-group–oriented programs are potentially much more cost

3. The expression for such elasticity is $\epsilon_p = \dfrac{\epsilon}{\alpha} + \left(\dfrac{1-\alpha}{\alpha}\right)\eta_R$, where α is the proportion of total food consumed by the target group.

4. The value of λ appears in the expression for the subsidy program, $\dfrac{1+\lambda}{\eta_p}$, as a result of evaluating the demand elasticity at initial values of prices and quantities. λ drops out if evaluated at final magnitudes. For small changes, $\lambda \to 0$, the expression tends to $1/\eta_p$.

Table 23. Cost Effectiveness of Target-Group–Oriented Programs and a General Food Price Subsidy Program with Different Demand and Supply Elasticities, as a Ratio of the Price per Unit [a]

Program	$\epsilon = \infty (\epsilon_p = \infty)$		$\epsilon = 1(\epsilon_p = 6.2)$		$\epsilon = 0.5(\epsilon_p = 3.7)$	
	η_p		η_p		η_p	
	1.0	0.5	1.0	0.5	1.0	0.5
Target group						
Food stamp	1.00	1.00	1.19	1.19	1.32	1.32
Price subsidy	1.20	2.40	1.39	2.59	1.52	2.72
Income transfer	2.00	2.00	2.39	2.19	2.65	2.32
General						
Price subsidy	5.45	11.40	7.85	15.28	10.25	19.25

a. The values of the other parameters are $\lambda = \alpha = 0.2$; $m = 0.5$; and $\eta_R = 0.3$.

effective and are probably the only feasible means to eliminate undernutrition in subgroups of the population. The difference in cost to the government is approximately between one to two times the price of the food for target-group–oriented programs and ten times that price for general price subsidies.

FEASIBILITY AND COST OF ACTUAL PROGRAMS

For target-group–oriented programs to be as effective as indicated in the previous sections, it must be possible to identify a homogeneous population with the characteristics described. Furthermore, it must be possible to implement the programs in a way that the benefits reach only the intended population. In reality these conditions are unlikely to be met. The cost effectiveness will tend to be less than maximum and minimum food consumption targets may not be reached.

Clearly, if the target group is fairly homogeneous with respect to income, its relative poverty is the decisive factor in making a choice between the programs. When the group is extremely poor, the price elasticity and the marginal propensity to consume food tend to approach 1, and the three programs are almost equally cost effective. Food stamps are more difficult to implement because participants would have to accumulate sufficient cash to purchase a month's or even a week's supply. If the target group's income and food consumption falls short only by a small fraction of adequate nutrition, the food stamp program might be twice as cost effective as the other programs.

If the target population is heterogeneous, some additional considerations enter. A price subsidy program aimed at the average income level is bound to lead the better-off members of the target group to consume beyond minimal nutritional requirements and to leave the poorest inadequately fed. A food stamp program in which everyone is charged the same amount for the stamps may have the result of preventing those in greatest need from participating, whereas it is less than fully cost effective for those with higher incomes. To avoid neglecting poorer members of the target group, charges for food stamps will have to be set liberally, which means the program will be less cost effective. A study by the U.S. Department of Agriculture reports that, on the average, participants of the U.S. Food Stamp Program spend 50 cents of each dollar of subsidy on food. In contrast, however, it is estimated that a direct income transfer would have provided only 20 cents worth of food consumption for every dollar.[5]

Still other factors must be considered when choosing among alternative programs. First, the foregoing comparisons of cost effectiveness do not take into account the value of additional nonfood expenditure induced by the transfer payment. For example, an income transfer might not be as cost effective as a food stamp program but would give the target population additional means for nonfood expenditure. Additional income might induce better health and lower fertility, both of which are complementary to food in reducing malnutrition.

Second, no food assistance can be expected to be totally efficient in the sense that the subsidized food reaches only the target group. Participating beneficiaries may not reveal the full truth of their circumstances and may receive unintended assistance. Middlemen and administrators may take illegal cuts and target-group beneficiaries may resell food intended to augment their own consumption. Thus, political and administrative problems may be as important as minor differences in cost effectiveness in determining the choice of an optimum program. Unless leakages are kept low, these inefficiencies will more than offset advantages perceived on the basis of idealized cost-effectiveness measures.

5. U.S., Department of Agriculture, Economic Research Service, "Bonus Food Stamps and Cash Income Supplements," Marketing Research Report no. 1034 (Washington, D.C., 1974).

Appendix A

Basic Country Data

THIS APPENDIX comprises a single table whose data indicate the basic figures for population, GNP per capita, and per capita daily calorie consumption—all from 1965—used throughout the main body of the book.

Table A.1. Population Distribution, per Capita Income, and per Capita Calorie Consumption, by Region and Country, 1965

Country	Population (thousands) (1)	GNP per capita [a] (1972 U.S. dollars) (2)	Per capita daily calorie consumption (3)
Latin America			
Argentina	22,545	1,069	2,868
Bolivia	4,334	179	1,731
Brazil	80,766	370	2,541
Chile	8,708	721	2,523
Colombia	18,020	343	2,220
Costa Rica	1,490	482	2,234
Cuba	7,631		2,665
Dominican Republic	3,624	360	2,004
Ecuador	5,150	302	1,848
El Salvador	2,917	315	1,877
Guatemala	4,581	365	1,952
Guyana	655	360	2,291
Haiti	4,396	118	1,904
Honduras	2,182	286	1,930
Jamaica	1,791	480	2,243
Mexico	42,689	470	2,623
Nicaragua	1,745	428	2,253
Panama	1,246	648	2,317
Paraguay	2,030	272	2,732
Peru	11,650	480	2,255

Table A.1 (*continued*)

Country	Population (thousands) (1)	GNP per capita [a] (1972 U.S. dollars) (2)	Per capita daily calorie consumption (3)
Puerto Rico	2,632		2,531
Surinam	338	566	2,371
Trinidad and Tobago	974	740	2,361
Uruguay	2,715	760	3,037
Venezuela	9,240	1,098	2,392
Total and average	244,049		2,471
Asia			
Burma	24,732	84	2,011
Sri Lanka	11,164	94	2,219
China, Republic of	12,962	301	2,379
Hong Kong	3,692	663	2,324
India	486,650	106	1,948
Indonesia	105,736	69	1,798
Khmer Republic	6,251	161	2,168
Korea, Republic of	28,377	180	2,421
Laos	2,631	104	2,005
Malaysia	9,422	352	2,255
Nepal	10,103	81	2,218
Pakistan	113,300	114	1,993
Philippines	32,345	188	1,895
Singapore	1,865	686	2,454
South Vietnam	16,124	178	2,134
Ceylon	11,164	94	2,219
Thailand	30,744	164	2,226
Total and average	869,098		1,984
Middle East			
Afghanistan	15,051	78	2,000
Cyprus	594	742	2,459
Iran	24,813	297	2,019
Iraq	8,140	328	2,055
Jordan	1,910	320	2,430
Lebanon	2,300	594	2,401
Libya	1,667	1,050	2,031
Saudi Arabia	4,500	349	2,077
Sudan	13,540	129	2,088
Syria	5,232	256	2,440
Turkey	31,151	274	2,858
United Arab Republic	29,389	229	2,421
Yemen, Arab Republic of	4,473		1,895
Yemen, People's Democratic Republic of	1,120	184	2,089
Total and average	143,880		2,315

Table A.1 *(continued)*

Country	Population (thousands) (1)	GNP per capita[a] (1972 U.S. dollars) (2)	Per capita daily calorie consumption (3)
Africa			
Algeria	11,923	318	1,967
Angola	5,154	214	1,907
Benin	2,365	73	2,230
Burundi	3,210	62	2,017
Cameroon	5,229	153	2,264
Central Africa Republic	1,335	139	2,172
Chad	3,307	93	2,259
Congo, Democratic Republic of	15,627	86	2,036
Congo, People's Republic of	840	268	2,151
Ethiopia	22,699	73	2,152
Gabon	463	548	2,164
Gambia, The	330	118	2,335
Ghana	7,740	257	2,136
Guinea	3,510		2,075
Ivory Coast	4,200	271	2,433
Kenya	9,365	131	2,253
Liberia	1,076	198	2,287
Malagasy Republic	6,059		2,375
Malawi	3,908	72	2,257
Mali	4,480	69	2,159
Mauritania	1,050	154	1,981
Mauritius	761	286	2,343
Morocco	13,323	226	2,091
Mozambique	6,957	212	2,108
Niger	3,513	100	2,211
Nigeria	58,480	102	2,168
Rwanda	3,110	53	1,908
Senegal	3,490	234	2,348
Sierra Leone	2,367	173	2,185
Somali	2,500	72	1,778
Southern Rhodesia	4,480	213	2,551
Tanzania	11,674	96	2,170
Togo	1,638	123	2,232
Tunisia	4,451	269	2,153
Uganda	7,551	85	2,179
Upper Volta	4,708	71	2,060
Zambia	3,710	356	2,237
Total and average	246,583		2,154

Sources: columns (1) and (3), Food and Agriculture Organization of the United Nations, *Agricultural Commodity Projects 1970–1980* (Rome, 1971); column (2), World Bank, Division of Economic and Social Data, Economic Analysis and Projections Department, average of 1964–66 period.

Appendix B

Income Distribution Data

ESTIMATION OF THE SHARES of the regional population in predetermined (dollar) per capita income ranges was made in two steps. First, the shares of the population in given dollar per capita income ranges were estimated for several countries in each region. Second, the corresponding shares of the region were then computed as the weighted average of the countries' shares, where the weights were the shares of the population of each country in the total population of the countries included in the sample. It was further assumed that the distribution of the countries excluded could be approximated with the regional distribution obtained with the countries included. The first step is discussed below; the regional distributions are reported in Table 4 in the text.

METHOD OF ESTIMATION

To estimate a country's population share in each income range, it is necessary to know the density function of the income distribution for each country. One approach has been to fit a Pareto or log normal function to actual observed data. The shortcoming of such an approach is that these density functions usually do not provide good statistical fits to the data. An alternative is to find an equation of the Lorenz curve that would fit actual data reasonably well. This curve has been estimated with a new technique, developed by Kakwani and Podder, that introduces a new coordinate system for the Lorenz curve and appears to fit actual data quite well.[1]

1. N. Kakwani and N. Podder, "Efficient Estimation of the Lorenz Curve and Associated Inequality Measures from Grouped Observations," *Econometrica*, 44 (January 1976): 137–48.

Figure B.1. A Typical Lorenz Curve Relation

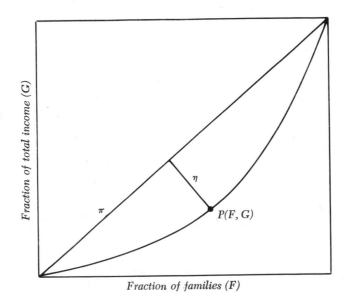

Fraction of families (F)

Figure B.1 represents a typical Lorenz curve relationship describing the percentage of families receiving specific fractions of total income. Families are ordered according to the per capita income of the family.

A given point $P(F,G)$ on the Lorenz curve defines the following coordinates:

(1)
$$\pi = \frac{F+G}{\sqrt{2}} \text{ and}$$

(2)
$$\eta = \frac{F-G}{\sqrt{2}}.$$

The Lorenz curve may be written in terms of these new coordinates as:

(3)
$$\eta = f(\pi),$$

where

(4)
$$\frac{d\eta}{d\pi} = \frac{\bar{\mu} - X}{\bar{\mu} + X},$$

where $\bar{\mu}$ is the mean household per capita income and X is any given per capita income of a family.[2]

A particular specification of the equation $\eta=f(\pi)$ is the form:

$$(5) \qquad \eta=a\,\pi^\alpha(\sqrt{2}-\pi)^\beta,$$

where the difference between α and β reflects the skewness of the Lorenz curve toward each extreme. For this particular specification equation (4) becomes:

$$(6) \qquad \alpha\,a\,\pi^{\alpha-1}\,(\sqrt{2}-\pi)^\beta-\beta\,a\,\pi^\alpha\,(\sqrt{2}-\pi)^{\beta-1}=\frac{\mu+X}{\mu-X}.$$

For estimation purposes, take logs of equation (5):

$$(7) \qquad \log\eta=\alpha'+\alpha\log\pi+\beta\log(\sqrt{2}-\pi).$$

Defining F_i as the cumulative percentage of families at the ith percentile ordered according to per capita household income, and G_i as the percentage of total income perceived by those F_i percentage of families:

$$(8) \qquad \pi_i=\frac{F_i+G_i}{\sqrt{2}},\text{ and}$$

$$(9) \qquad \eta_i=\frac{F_i-G_i}{\sqrt{2}}.$$

The estimating equation therefore becomes:

$$(10) \qquad \log\eta_i=\alpha'+\alpha\log\pi_i+\beta\log(\sqrt{2}-\pi_i)+\mu_i.$$

DATA AND RESULTS

The basic income distribution data and data sources are presented in Tables B.1–B.4.[3] Equation (10) was estimated for each country

---

2. Equation (4) is derived as follows:

$g(X)=$ density function of X,

$$F(X)=\int_0^X X\,g(X)dX=\text{fraction of families below per capita income }X,\text{ and}$$

$$G(X)=\frac{1}{\mu}\int_0^X Xg(X)dX=\text{fraction of total income of families below per}$$

capita income X.

Equation (4) is then obtained by making use of the derivatives $d\pi/dF$, $d\pi/dG$, $d\eta/dF$, $d\eta/dG$, $F'(X)$, and $G'(X)$.

3. The data were provided by Shail Jain of the Income Distribution Division, Development Research Center, the World Bank. See also Shail Jain, *Size Distribution of Income: A Compilation of Data* (Washington, D.C.: World Bank, 1976).

using ordinary least squares. Table B.5 gives the values of the parameters a, α, and β for each country. The coefficient of determination (R^2) of all regressions yielded values over 0.98.

Substituting the values of the estimated parameters into equation (6), and given the mean per capita income of the country (μ), it is possible to solve for π, given X. The value of π can then be substituted into (5) so as to derive the corresponding value for η.

By the above procedure the values of F and G for any predetermined per capita income X are obtained. Basically we are interested in F given X, the percentage of families with per capita household income below X. The results for thirty countries are reported in Tables B.6 and B.7.

Table B.1 Africa: Income Distribution Data, Selected Countries, Various Years [a]
(Cumulative percentages)

Chad, 1958		Gabon, 1968		Ivory Coast, 1959		Malawi, 1969	
Population	Income	Income recipients	Income	Population	Income	Households	Income
60	35	10	1.4	60	30	10	2.3
80	57	20	3.3	80	45	20	5.8
90	70	30	5.8	90	60	30	10.0
95	77	40	8.8	95	80	40	14.9
100	100	50	12.0	100	100	50	20.9
		60	16.7			60	28.2
		70	23.5			70	36.8
		80	32.5			80	46.8
		90	45.5			90	60.8
		95	54.9			95	70.8
		100	100.0			100	100.0

Senegal, 1960	
Population	Income
20	3
40	10
60	20
80	36
90	52
95	64
100	100

Tanzania, 1967	
Population	Income
20	5.0
40	13.5
60	25.0
80	40.0
90	55.0
95	66.0
100	100.0

Uganda, 1970	
Adult male employees	Income
2.3	0.3
11.4	2.9
18.0	5.3
23.4	7.8
41.2	17.9
55.0	27.2
61.6	32.3
75.4	46.6
84.7	60.1
90.9	71.7
100.0	100.0

Sources: Chad, Gabon, Ivory Coast, and Senegal, Christian Morrisson, *La répartition des revenus dans les pays du tiers-monde* (Paris: Editions Cujas, 1969); Malawi, Christian Morrisson, "Special Paper on Malawi" (Washington, D.C.: World Bank, Income Distribution Division, 1973; unpublished memorandum; Tanzania, 'Annual Economic Survey of 1968–69," in Christian Morrisson, "Special Paper on Tanzania" (Washington, D.C.: World Bank, Income Distribution Division, 1973; unpublished memorandum); Uganda, Ministry of Planning and Economic Development, Statistics Division, *Enumeration of Employees, 1961–1970* (Entebbe: Uganda Government Printer, annual).

a. The surveyed categories "Population," "Income recipients," "Households," and so on are variously defined in the sources.

Table B.2 Asia: Income Distribution Data, Selected Countries, Various Years *
(Cumulative percentages)

Hong Kong, 1971		India, 1964–65		Korea, 1970	
Households	Income	Families	Income	Families	Income
4.8	0.7	10	3.3	20	7
15.3	3.9	20	7.7	40	18
39.3	15.9	30	13.0	60	33
59.0	28.8	40	19.1	80	55
70.3	40.4	50	26.0	90	72
79.8	50.5	60	34.1	95	83
87.1	60.4	70	43.1	100	100
91.8	68.7	80	53.9		
95.1	76.1	90	70.0		
98.3	87.3	100	100.0		
100.0	100.0				

Malaysia, 1970		Pakistan, 1970–71		Philippines, 1965	
Households	Income	Households	Income	Families	Income
6.40	0.40	0.4	0.1	20	3.6
9.54	0.88	9.4	3.3	40	11.6
20.53	3.58	32.3	15.4	60	24.4
28.11	6.16	53.4	30.9	80	44.6
38.95	10.88	68.5	45.2	90	60.0
45.33	14.26	79.4	57.8	100	100.0
54.33	19.88	90.5	73.9		
59.14	23.34	94.7	81.8		
73.63	36.50	98.1	90.4		
75.95	39.05	99.0	93.7		
84.64	50.56	99.6	96.5		
88.63	57.25	99.9	98.4		
89.30	58.50	100.0	100.0		
92.07	64.21				
93.72	68.18				
94.00	68.90				
94.64	70.65				
95.13	72.08				
96.11	75.23				
96.68	77.25				
100.00	100.00				

Sources: Hong Kong, Census and Statistics Department, Hong Kong Population and Housing Census 1971, Main Report (Hong Kong: Government Printer, 1973); India, K. R. Ranadive, in Pranab K. Bardhan, "The Pattern of Income Distribution in India: A Review" (Washington, D.C.: World Bank, Development Research Center 1973: processed); Korea, Bureau of Statistics, Economic Planning Board, Annual Report of the Family Income and Expenditure Survey, (Seoul, 1970) and Korea, Ministry of Agriculture and Forestry, Report on the Results of Farm Household Economy Survey and Production Cost Survey of Agricultural Products (Seoul, 1971); Malaysia, Department of Statistics, "Post Enumeration Survey of 1970 Census" (unpublished report); Pakistan, Ministry of Finance, Planning and Development, Statistical Division Household Income and Expenditure Survey 1970–71 (Karachi: Government Publications Division, n.d.); Philippines, Department of Commerce and Industry, Bureau of Census and Statistics, "Family Income and Expenditure 1961, 1965, and 1971," BCS Survey of Households Bulletin, nos. 14, 22, and 34 (Manila, 1964, 1968, and 1973).
a. The surveyed categories "Households" and "Families" are variously defined in the sources.

Table B.3 Middle East: Income Distribution Data, Selected Countries, Various Years [a]
(Cumulative percentages)

Egypt, 1964–65		Iraq, 1956		Libya, 1962		Sudan, 1963		Tunisia, 1970	
Households	Income	Population	Income	Households	Income	Households	Income	Recipients	Income
32.6	9.7	60	16	2.1	0.8	10	2.0	10	1.8
63.2	32.5	80	32	11.8	5.5	20	5.2	20	4.1
83.6	57.9	90	49	26.0	13.9	30	9.5	30	7.2
91.8	72.2	95	66	48.6	30.3	40	14.2	40	11.4
100.0	100.0	100	100	66.7	47.5	50	20.3	50	16.6
				81.6	65.3	60	28.0	60	23.4
				89.9	77.6	70	37.2	70	32.4
				96.2	88.9	80	49.2	80	45.0
				100.0	100.0	90	66.8	90	62.4
						100	100.0	100	100.0

Sources: Egypt, United Arab Republic Institute, *Report on Employment Problems in Rural Areas* (Cairo, 1968) and Mostafa H. Nagi, *Labor Force and Employment in Egypt: A Demographic and Socioeconomic Analysis* (New York: Praeger, 1971); Iraq, Christian Morrisson, *La Répartition des revenues dans les pays du tiers-monde* (Paris: Editions Cujas, 1969); Libya, Libyan Arab Republic, Ministry of National Economy, Central Statistics Office, *Family Budget Survey in Tripoli Town, 1962* (Tripoli, 1963); Sudan, Department of Statistics, *Omdurman Household Budget Survey* (Khartoum, 1965); Tunisia, Christian Morrisson, "Special Paper on Tunisia," (unpublished memorandum) (Washington, D.C.: World Bank, Income Distribution Division, 1973) and Tunoisia, Premier Ministère, Institut National de la Statistique, *La consummation et les dépenses des ménages en Tunisie, 1965–68* (Tunis, 1970).

a. The surveyed categories "Households," "Population," and "Recipients" are variously defined in the sources.

Table B.4 Latin America: Income Distribution Data, Selected Countries, Various Years [a]
(Cumulative percentages)

Brazil, 1970 Economically active population	Income	Chile, 1968 Families	Income	Colombia, 1970 Population	Income	Costa Rica, 1971 Families	Income
10	1.17	10	2	20	1.5	10	2.1
20	3.49	20	4.5	40	9.4	20	5.4
30	6.91	30	8.5	60	22.0	30	9.6
40	11.56	40	13.0	80	40.5	40	14.7
50	17.71	50	18.9	95	67.5	50	20.9
60	25.37	60	25.7	100	100.0	60	28.4
70	34.78	70	33.8			70	37.7
80	45.63	80	43.2			80	49.4
90	60.32	90	58.0			90	65.6
95	72.29	95	69.6			95	77.2
100	100.00	100	100.0			100	100.0

Table B.4 (continued)

Dominican Republic, 1969		El Salvador, 1965–67 Economically active population		Guatemala, 1966 Households		Honduras, 1967–68	
Families	Income	population	Income	Households	Income	Families	Income
5.1	0.6	10	2.4	2.8	0.8	33.8	4.8
23.2	5.6	20	5.5	8.8	3.2	52.9	11.3
53.3	20.3	30	8.7	19.7	8.8	62.7	17.1
71.6	35.6	40	12.0	33.4	17.3	69.7	23.0
81.9	47.9	50	16.0	45.7	26.3	76.5	30.5
90.4	62.2	60	20.8	55.8	34.8	80.7	36.0
93.6	70.0	70	28.0	64.0	42.6	84.7	42.2
95.8	76.7	80	38.6	71.1	50.1	86.0	45.8
100.0	100.0	90	54.4	76.6	56.5	89.9	54.4
		95	67.0	80.9	62.0	92.4	61.1
		99	82.0	84.3	66.8	94.1	66.3
		100	100.0	86.8	70.5	95.0	69.4
				88.8	73.7	95.6	72.0
				90.4	76.5	96.3	75.4
				92.1	79.7	97.0	79.3
				93.8	82.9	100.0	100.0
				94.8	85.0		
				95.4	86.2		
				97.1	90.1		
				98.6	94.2		
				99.2	96.2		
				99.8	98.6		
				100.0	100.0		

Jamaica, 1958		Panama, 1969		Peru, 1961 Economically active		Uruguay, 1967 Employed	
Households	Income	Active population	Income	population	Income	population	Income
20	2.2	23.0	3.7	10	1.0	10	1.0
30	4.7	45.5	12.3	20	2.5	20	2.9
40	8.2	64.8	25.5	30	4.7	30	5.7
50	12.9	77.7	38.0	40	8.0	40	10.0
60	19.0	84.5	46.6	50	12.3	50	16.2
70	27.3	90.9	57.6	60	18.2	60	24.4
80	38.5	96.3	71.9	70	25.8	70	34.5
90	56.5	98.6	81.8	80	35.6	80	47.4
95	69.8	99.5	89.3	90	50.8	90	64.3
100	100.0	99.8	94.7	95	61.0	100	100.0
		100.0	100.0	100	100.0		

Sources: Brazil, Carlos G. Langoni, "Distribuição da Renda e Desenvolvimento Econômico de Brasil (Rio de Janeiro: Editora Expressão e Cultura, 1973); Chile, Dirección General de Estadística y Censos, *Encuesta Nacional sobre Ingresos Familiares, Serie de Investigaciones Muestrales* (Santiago, June 1969); Colombia, Departamento Administrativo Nacional de Estadística, *Encuesta de Hogares de Propósitos Múltiples: Encuesta de Hogares 1970* (Bogotá, June, 1971) and *Encuesta de Hogares 1970: Análisis de Ingresos* (Bogota, February, 1971); Costa Rica, Universidad de Costa Rica, "*La Distribución del Ingreso y del Consumo de Algunos Alimentos*" (San José, September 1972); Dominican Republic, Banco Central, Oficina Nacional de Estadísticas—Agencia Internacional para el Desarrollo, *Estudio sobre Presupuestos Familiares,* vol. 1: *Ingresos y las familias en la ciudad de Santo Domingo, 1969* (Santo Domingo, 1961); El Salvador, United Nations Economic Commission for Latin America, *Economic Survey of Latin America, 1968* part one (E/CN. 12/825 Rev. 1) (New York: United Nations, 1969); Guatemala, R. A. Orellana Gonzáles, *Encuesta sobre Ingresos y Gastos de la Familia del Campesino Asalariado de Guatemala* (Guatemala City, 1966); Honduras, Dirección de Estadísticas y Censos, *Encuesta de Ingresos y Gastos Familiares 1967–68* (Tegucigalpa, April, 1970); Jamaica, E. Ahiram, "Income Distribution in Jamaica, 1958," *Social and Economic Studies,* vol. 13, no. 3 (September 1964), pp. 333–70 (Jamaica: University of the West Indies, Institute of Social and Economic Research); Panama, Charles C. McLure, Jr., "The Distribution of Income and Tax Incidence in Panama, 1969," Working Paper no. 36 (Houston, Tex.: Rice University, Program of Development Studies); Peru, Richard Webb, "The Distribution of Income in Peru," Discussion Paper no. 26 (Princeton, N.J.: Woodrow Wilson School, Princeton University, 1972); Uruguay, Universidad de la República, Instituto de Economía, *La Distribución del Ingreso en Uruguay,* Documento de Referencia no. 6 (Santiago: Facultad de Ciencias Económicas y de Administración, 1971).

a. The surveyed categories "Economically active population," "Families," "Population," and so on are defined variously in the sources.

Table B.5.   Estimates of the Parameters of the Lorenz Curve

Region and country	a	α	β
Asia			
Hong Kong	0.386	0.879	0.786
India	0.351	0.871	0.663
Korea, Republic of	0.366	0.949	0.901
Malaysia	0.485	0.899	0.849
Pakistan	0.294	0.887	0.770
Philippines	0.465	0.875	0.807
Africa			
Chad	0.315	0.877	0.700
Gabon	0.679	1.002	0.853
Ivory Coast	0.372	0.893	0.614
Malawi	0.411	0.912	0.715
Senegal	0.568	0.969	0.850
Tanzania	0.457	0.945	0.756
Uganda	0.369	0.888	0.829
Middle East			
Iraq	0.697	1.047	1.042
Libya	0.249	0.919	0.821
Sudan	0.437	0.927	0.913
Tunisia	0.533	1.006	0.999
United Arab Republic	0.413	0.875	0.908
Latin America			
Brazil	0.576	0.978	0.910
Chile	0.465	0.939	0.780
Colombia	0.557	0.983	0.904
Costa Rica	0.421	0.921	0.850
Dominican Republic	0.472	0.929	0.867
El Salvador	0.536	0.950	0.921
Guatemala	0.270	0.875	0.799
Honduras	0.661	0.993	1.021
Jamaica	0.585	0.949	0.960
Panama	0.533	0.925	0.868
Peru	0.606	0.978	0.886
Uruguay	0.394	0.834	0.883

Source: Calculated from data in Tables B.1.–B.4.

Table B.6. Estimates of the Country Distribution of Population by per Capita Income Ranges: Africa, Asia, and Middle East
(Percentages)

Country	Per capita income in 1965 (1972 U.S. dollars)							
	0–50	50–100	100–150	150–200	200–250	250–300	300–350	350+
Africa								
Chad	25.0	47.6	16.8	5.9	2.4	1.1	0.6	0.6
Gabon	9.3	15.9	12.2	9.6	7.7	6.2	5.1	34.0
Ivory Coast	1.0	11.8	24.5	20.1	13.6	9.0	6.0	14.0
Malawi	53.6	31.4	9.0	3.3	1.4	0.7	0.3	0.3
Senegal	17.6	25.1	16.2	10.7	7.3	5.2	3.7	14.2
Tanzania	42.2	33.2	12.6	5.6	2.8	1.5	0.9	1.2
Uganda	22.7	38.0	18.9	9.3	4.8	2.5	1.4	2.4
Asia								
Hong Kong	0.6	1.2	2.9	5.4	7.3	8.0	7.9	66.7
India	23.4	45.2	18.1	7.1	3.1	1.5	0.9	0.7
Korea, Republic of	2.2	30.3	23.0	14.5	9.4	6.3	4.3	10.0
Malaysia	6.1	13.4	14.5	12.3	9.8	7.7	6.1	30.1
Pakistan	10.4	46.0	24.0	10.4	4.6	2.1	1.0	1.5
Philippines	16.3	25.9	18.7	12.1	7.9	5.2	3.6	10.3
Middle East								
Iraq	20.0	10.0	21.7	8.7	6.4	4.9	3.9	24.4
Libya	0	0	0	0	0.01	0.1	0.2	97.6
Sudan	24.0	31.6	17.2	9.7	5.9	3.7	2.4	5.5
Tunisia	11.0	20.0	16.0	11.0	8.0	6.0	5.0	23.0
United Arab Republic	7.8	19.0	18.1	13.7	10.0	7.3	5.5	18.6

Table B.7. Estimates of the Country Distribution of Population by per Capita Income Ranges: Latin America
(Percentages)

Country	Per capita income in 1965 (1972 U.S. dollars)												
	0–50	50–100	100–150	150–200	200–250	250–300	300–350	350–400	400–500	500–600	600–800	800–1,000	1,000+
Brazil	7.3	18.5	14.5	10.9	8.4	6.5	5.2	4.1	6.1	4.2	5.2	2.9	6.2
Chile	0.1	1.0	4.4	8.0	9.0	8.5	7.7	6.8	11.1	8.5	11.7	7.2	16.0
Colombia	5.4	20.5	15.6	11.5	8.6	6.6	5.1	4.1	5.9	4.0	4.8	2.7	5.2
Costa Rica	0.4	3.4	9.5	11.6	10.8	9.3	7.9	6.6	10.2	7.3	9.1	5.1	8.8
Dominican Republic	2.8	13.2	15.3	12.8	10.1	8.0	6.3	5.0	7.4	5.0	5.9	3.1	5.1
El Salvador	8.9	18.5	15.1	11.3	8.5	6.6	5.1	4.0	5.9	4.0	4.7	2.6	4.8
Guatemala	0.1	0.8	5.1	13.1	15.6	14.0	11.4	9.1	12.6	7.4	6.8	2.3	1.7
Honduras	23.0	18.0	12.4	8.8	6.5	5.0	3.9	3.1	4.5	3.1	3.8	2.2	5.6
Jamaica	5.9	9.0	9.2	8.3	7.2	6.3	5.4	4.7	7.7	5.9	8.4	5.5	16.5
Panama	3.2	6.4	8.6	8.7	8.0	7.1	6.2	5.4	8.9	6.8	9.4	6.0	15.4
Peru	6.1	15.2	12.9	10.3	8.2	6.7	5.4	4.5	6.9	3.6	8.9	7.3	4.0
Uruguay	2.2	1.9	3.0	4.1	5.0	5.5	5.7	5.6	10.4	9.0	13.9	9.7	24.0

Appendix C

Estimated Calorie Consumption Functions Based on Cross-country Data

It is generally observed that income elasticities decline as income increases. For instance, in Table C.1 are the calorie elasticities implied by FAO projections of food consumption, which in turn are based on an examination of a large number of food demand studies.

In theory, many functional forms could be used to specify a calorie-income equation that yields declining calorie elasticities as income rises. In regressing country per capita calorie consumption and income data, several such functional forms of the equation have been estimated, as well as the constant elasticity equation. The estimated functions and corresponding elasticity equations are as follows:

$$
\begin{array}{lll}
\text{Semilog:} & C = a + b\mathrm{Ln}X & \mu = b/C \\
\text{Inverse:} & C = a + b(1/X) & \mu = -b/C \cdot X \\
\text{Double log:} & \mathrm{Ln}C = a + b\mathrm{Ln}X & \mu = b \\
\text{Log inverse:} & \mathrm{Ln}C = a + b(1/X) & \mu = -b/X
\end{array}
$$

The statistical results as well as the implied elasticities and daily calorie consumption at two extreme levels of income are shown in Table C.2.

Whereas on statistical goodness-of-fit criteria there is little basis for choosing between the functional forms, the estimates of elasticities and consumption levels at extreme levels of income show that some functional forms are more plausible than others. The estimated parameters in the inverse and log-inverse function, for instance, imply that calorie consumption does not exceed 2,600 calories at any income level in all regions. This does not seem plausible. Furthermore, the inverse functions imply too low consumption levels at a low per capita income level in Latin America; in fact, the inverse function implies negative consumption. Given these considerations of plausibility and the a priori preference for a function that specifies declining elasticity as income rises, the semilog form was chosen as providing the best representation of the calorie consumption function.

Table C.1. Average per Capita Private Consumption Expenditure and Income Elasticities of Demand for Food, Selected Regions and Countries, 1964–66

Geographic areas/countries	Per capita private consumption expenditure (U.S. dollars, constant 1972 prices)	Income elasticities of demand for all food expressed in	
		Calories	Total proteins
South Asia	75	0.39	0.37
East Africa	78	0.32	0.36
Central Africa	81	0.31	0.21
West Africa	94	0.32	0.41
East and Southeast Asia	119	0.23	0.30
Northwest Africa	158	0.40	0.35
Middle East	183	0.15	0.15
Latin America	342	0.19	0.19
Eastern Europe	553	0.02	0.09
Japan	603	0.13	0.19
Israel	942	0.06	0.13
Western Europe	1,050	0.06	0.11
North America	2,611	−0.01	0.00

Source: Compiled from Table 8 and Table B in Part II, Statistical Appendix of Volume II, FAO, Agricultural Commodity Projections 1970–1980 (Rome, 1971).

Table C.2. Cross-country Data, 1965, Based on Regressions of Daily per Capita Calorie Consumption (C) on per Capita Income (X)

Region and form of equation	Equation [a]	R^2	Elasticity		Calorie consumption	
			X=US$25	X=US$2,000	X=US$25	X=US$2,000
Latin America						
Semilog	C=256+417 LnX (4.1)	0.44	0.260	0.122	1,598	3,425
Inverse	C=2,594−117,979(1/X) (−3.3)	0.34	2.221	0.023	<0	2,535
Double log	LnC=6.58+0.19 LnX (4.3)	0.47	0.190	0.190	1,335	3,050
Log-inverse	LnC=7.86−54(1/X) (−3.5)	0.37	2.160	0.027	300	2,520
Asia						
Semilog	C=1,191+188 LnX (3.5)	0.46	0.105	0.07	1,796	2,620
Inverse	C=2,390−32,900(1/X) (−3.4)	0.45	1.224	0.01	1,075	2,375
Double log	LnC=7.22+.09 LnX (3.4)	0.45	0.090	0.09	1,825	2,708
Log-inverse	LnC=7.78−15.4(1/X) (−3.4)	0.45	0.616	0.01	1,292	2,373

Table C.2 (continued)

Region and form of equation	Equation [a]	R^2	Elasticity		Calorie consumption	
			X=US$25	X=US$2,000	X=US$25	X=US$2,000
Middle East						
Semilog	$C = 1,857 + 71 \, LnX$ (0.6)	0.04	0.034	0.030	2,082	2,394
Inverse	$C = 2,368 - 26,080(1/X)$ (−1.1)	0.10	0.787	0.006	1,325	2,355
Double log	$LnC = 7.53 - .03 \, LnX$ (0.7)	0.04	0.030	0.030	2,050	2,340
Log-inverse	$LnC = 7.77 - 11.6(1/X)$ (−1.2)	0.11	0.465	0.006	1,490	2,355
Africa						
Semilog	$C = 1.700 + 96 \, LnX$ (2.4)	0.15	0.048	0.040	2,009	2,424
Inverse	$C = 2,298 - 14,736(1/X)$ (−2.9)	0.20	0.345	0.003	1,710	2,290
Double log	$LnC = 7.46 + .05 \, LnX$ (2.4)	0.15	0.050	0.050	2,040	2,540
Log-inverse	$LnC = 7.74 - 6.89(1/X)$ (−1.9)	0.21	0.276	0.003	1,745	2,290

a. Figures in parentheses are *t*-statistics.

Appendix D

Projected Calorie Deficits

THE CALCULATIONS discussed in Chapter 2 are amplified here. Population projections by income groups in each region appear in Table D.1. Estimated calorie deficits with alternative consumption functions are given in Table D.2. Daily per capita calorie deficit estimates in the affected population by region, for 1975 and 1990, are shown in Table D.3.

Table D.1. Projected Population by Income Group and Region, 1965, 1975, and 1990
(Millions)

Income group	Latin America			Asia			Middle East			Africa			Total population		
	1965	1975	1990	1965	1975	1990	1965	1975	1990	1965	1975	1990	1965	1975	1990
I	16	21	30	176	221	311	19	24	35	73	93	135	284	359	511
II	39	50	72	387	486	683	29	37	54	78	100	145	533	673	954
III	32	41	59	173	217	305	26	33	48	39	50	72	270	341	484
IV	26	33	48	74	93	131	16	21	30	21	27	39	137	174	248
V	21	27	39	36	45	64	12	15	22	12	15	22	81	102	147
VI	17	22	32	19	24	34	8	10	15	7	9	13	51	65	94
VII	14	18	26	12	15	21	6	8	11	5	6	9	37	47	67
VIII	79	101	146	19	24	34	27	35	50	11	14	20	136	174	250
Total	244	313	452	896	1,125	1,583	143	183	265	246	314	455	1,529	1,935	2,755

Source: United Nations Population Division, "Trends and Prospects in Urban and Rural Populations" (New York, April 1975).

Table D.2. Estimated Daily Calorie Deficit, by Income Group and Region, 1965

Region and income group	Calorie income elasticity=0.15		Calorie income elasticity=0.30	
	Per capita	Total (thousand millions)	Per capita	Total (thousand millions)
Latin America				
I	643	10.3	1,365	22.0
II	369	14.4	818	31.9
III	186	5.9	452	14.3
IV	65	1.7	211	5.5
Asia				
I	539	94.6	850	149.3
II	286	110.6	345	133.6
III	116	20.1	0	0
Middle East				
I	687	13.2	1,236	23.8
II	406	11.9	676	19.8
III	218	5.6	300	7.6
IV	94	1.6	53	0.9
Africa				
I	521	38.1	845	61.8
II	252	19.7	308	24.1
III	72	2.8	0	0

Table D.3. Estimated Daily per Capita Calorie Deficit in Affected Population, by Income Group and Region, 1975 and 1990

| Region and income group | 1965 | Daily calorie deficit by year and projection alternative | | | | | |
| | | 1975 | | | 1990 | | |
		A	B	C	A	B	C
Latin America							
I	643	571	535	489	463	374	245
II	369	297	261	208	189	100	0
III	186	114	78	20	0	0	0
IV	65	0	0	0	0	0	0
Asia							
I	539	506	473	429	456	373	255
II	286	253	220	170	203	120	0
III	116	83	50	0	33	0	0
Middle East							
I	687	577	467	417	411	135	0
II	406	296	186	129	130	0	0
III	218	108	0	0	0	0	0
IV	94	0	0	0	0	0	0
Africa							
I	521	486	451	404	433	355	227
II	252	217	182	128	167	86	0
III	72	37	0	0	0	0	0

Appendix E

Cost of Programs Oriented to Target Groups

ASSUME THAT Figure E.1 represents the food market relevant for the target group; D_p represents the demand by the target (poorer) group as a function of initial income Y; and S_p represents the (excess) supply faced by the group. That supply is equal to the total supply, S_T, minus the demand by the nontarget (richer) group, D_R. Initial consumption and price is F_o and P_o, respectively.

The object is to induce an increase in food consumption equal to ΔF: that is, the goal is an increase equal to $\lambda = \Delta F / F_o$. Some basic expressions are first derived that later will be used in computing the cost of these alternative options.

—The change (increase) in price necessary to induce an increment in supply equal to ΔF. Such an increase is equal to Δ_1. Denoting by ϵ_p the elasticity of supply faced by the target group, the following expression may be defined:

(1)
$$\frac{\Delta_1}{P_o} = \frac{\lambda}{\epsilon_p}.$$

—The change (decline) in price required to induce the target group to increase consumption by λ. That change is equal to Δ_2. Denoting by η_p the price elasticity of demand of the target group, the following expression may be defined (in absolute value):

(2)
$$\frac{\Delta_2}{P_o} = \frac{\lambda}{\eta_p}.$$

—The change (decline) in consumption because of the increase in price defined in equation (1), Δ_1. Such a decline is equal to Δ_3.

79

Figure E.1. Analysis of the Food Market Relevant for the Target Group

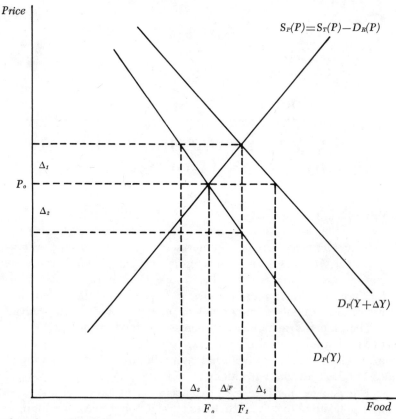

Therefore, the following expression may be written (in absolute value):

$$(3) \qquad \frac{\Delta_3}{F_o} = \lambda \frac{\eta_p}{\epsilon_p}.$$

COST OF AN INCOME TRANSFER

What is the value of ΔY—the income transfer—required to induce an increase in consumption by a fraction λ?

Denoting as m the marginal propensity to spend in food:

$$(4) \qquad m\Delta Y = P_o(\Delta F + \Delta_4) \text{ and}$$

$$(5) \qquad \Delta Y = \frac{P_o}{m}(\Delta F + \Delta_4).$$

Multiplying and dividing by $F_1 = F_o + \Delta F$:

$$(6) \qquad \Delta Y = \frac{P_o}{m}(F_o + \Delta F)\left[\frac{\Delta F}{F_o + \Delta F} + \frac{\Delta_4}{F_1}\right].$$

For small changes, $\frac{\Delta_4}{F_1} \simeq \frac{\Delta_3}{F_o}$, so substituting from equation (3) and dividing by ΔF gives:

$$(7) \qquad C_T = \frac{\Delta Y}{\Delta F} = \frac{P_o}{m}\left[1 + (1+\lambda)\frac{\eta_p}{\epsilon_p}\right].$$

C_T represents the cost of the income transfer per unit increment in food consumption induced by that transfer.

COST OF A PRICE SUBSIDY

If it is possible to subsidize the consumption of the target group—without subsidizing the nontarget group—the cost of the subsidy is equal to:

$$(8) \qquad (F_o + \Delta F)(\Delta_1 + \Delta_2).$$

Substituting from equations (1) and (2):

$$(9) \qquad (F_o + \Delta F)\,\lambda\,P\left[\frac{1}{\epsilon_p} + \frac{1}{\eta_p}\right].$$

Dividing by ΔF:

$$(10) \qquad C_S = P(1+\lambda)\left[\frac{1}{\epsilon_p} + \frac{1}{\eta_p}\right].$$

C_S represents the fiscal cost of the subsidy per unit increment in food consumption by the target group.

COST OF A FOOD STAMP PROGRAM

The suboptimal food stamp program described in the text is designed in such a way that the value of the additional food consumption is equal to the fiscal cost (transfer) of the program. The question is: What is the value of that transfer required to induce an increment in physical consumption equal to ΔF?

The value of the transfer must be able to finance the increment ΔF—valued at the new supply price of the commodity—as well as to finance the increased cost of old consumption. The transfer becomes equal to:

(11) $$\Delta F(P_o + \Delta_1) + F_o \Delta_1 \text{ or}$$

(12) $$\frac{P_o}{P_o} \Delta_1 (F_o + \Delta F) + P_o \Delta F.$$

Substituting Δ_1 from (1):

(13) $$P_o\left(\frac{\lambda}{\epsilon_p}\right)(F_o + \Delta F) + P_o \Delta F.$$

Dividing by ΔF gives:

(14) $$C_{St} = P_o\left[\frac{1+\lambda}{\epsilon_p} + 1\right]$$

C_{St} represents the cost of the program per unit increment in food consumption by the target group.